THE DOGS

SURREY COUNTY COUNCIL
WITHDRAWN FROM STOCK
AND APPROVED FOR SALE
WITH ALL FAULTS.
Price......30.........p

*By the same author
in this Series*

Earlier

THE GARDENS OF CAMELOT
THE ALTAR IN THE LOFT
THE DRUMS OF MORNING
THE GLITTERING PASTURES
THE NUMBERS CAME
THE LAST OF SPRING
THE PURPLE STREAK
THE WILD HILLS
THE HAPPY HIGHWAYS
THE SOUND OF REVELRY
THE MOON IN MY POCKET
THE BLOOD-RED ISLAND
THE GORGEOUS EAST
THE LICENTIOUS SOLDIERY

Later

THE LIFE FOR ME
THE VERDICT OF YOU ALL
THE TANGERINE HOUSE
THE QUEST FOR QUIXOTE
THE WINTRY SEA
THE GHOST OF JUNE

Supplementary

THE WORLD IS YOUNG
THE MAN IN EUROPE STREET
THE CIRCUS HAS NO HOME

The Dogs of Peace

RUPERT CROFT-COOKE

W. H. ALLEN . LONDON & NEW YORK
A division of Howard & Wyndham Ltd
1973

© RUPERT CROFT-COOKE, 1973
THIS BOOK OR PARTS THEREOF MAY NOT BE
REPRODUCED WITHOUT PERMISSION IN WRITING
PRINTED AND BOUND IN GREAT BRITAIN BY
BUTLER AND TANNER LTD, LONDON AND FROME
FOR THE PUBLISHERS W. H. ALLEN & CO LTD
43 ESSEX STREET LONDON WC2R 3JG
ISBN 0 491 00864 3

Contents

	Forenote	7
One	Welcome Home	11
Two	Litigation and Reviewing	27
Three	Last of the Gypsies	47
Four	Outsiders and 'In' People	66
Five	Merry Hall and Taconeo	89
Six	Abroad	107
Seven	The Wheatsheaf	120
Eight	Round the Peninsula	135
Nine	A Collection of Episodes	148
Ten	Cinema and Bullring	170
	L'Envoi	189

Forenote

As USUAL with the books in this series, this one is entirely independent of the others and can be read without previous knowledge of them.

It tells of those very strange years immediately after the Second World War, when I came back from India to settle in London and made several interesting journeys from there. I have been accused of name-dropping and since at this period I met most of the public figures I have known, and who seem to me likely to interest the reader, I make no apology for it. I am reminded of the American film-star who said—'I *hate* all this name-dropping. It's in *such* bad taste. I was only saying to the Queen last Thursday . . .'

This is the twenty-first of this series of books and ties up the rest in due order leaving only two to complete the whole task I set myself fifteen years ago—that of telling the story of a fairly eventful life stretching through most of the century, which has had no great importance except to its chronicler. It admits to being comprehensive and at times trivial, rather than selective. It might have taken less time if I had been able to dedicate myself entirely to it but unfortunately I could not have kept alive without other, less subjective forms of writing in the meantime.

The remaining two books will chronicle first the last ten of the fourteen years I spent in Morocco, after those covered in *The Tangerine House*, and apart from *The Quest for Quixote*, *The Wintry Sea* and *The Ghost of June*. It will probably be called *The Caves of Hercules*, while the very last (unless senility or death become unduly delayed) will be one which tells how I attempted to make six homes, in Normandy, the Canary Isles, Gibraltar, Cyprus, Tunis, and the Irish Republic, and finally settled not far from Tangier, my starting-point, in the Spanish North African part of Ceuta. The entire book (and my hope, a remote one, is to see it issued *as* a book, edited and illustrated) will if it is completed, run to some two million words, and will be called *The Sensual World*. In this I have been encouraged by a number of reviewers, not least by one of those anonymous writers in *The Times Literary Supplement* (not usually a generous critical organ), who said I had 'an almost faultless sense of period and a most endearing ability to recall factual details. Social historians of the future will do well to consult Mr Croft-Cooke's in preference to certain other more pretentious and less objective memoirs of the period'.

So I append here a list of the entire sequence, *The Sensual World*, giving dates of the periods covered in each book and the backgrounds of some of the chapters in them:

The Gardens of Camelot 1903–1914. Lindfield, Chipstead, Banstead.

The Altar in the Loft 1914–1917. Tonbridge, Hastings.

The Drums of Morning 1917–1920. Aldenham, Eastbourne, Wellington (Salop), Kessingland, Norfolk Broads, New Brighton, Liverpool, Lytham.

The Glittering Pastures 1920–1925. Hastings, Hove, Paris, Le Touquet, Aix-les-Bains, Steyning, Sevenoaks, Burwash, London SW23, Buenos Aires, San Isidro.

The Numbers Came 1925–1929. New Barn, London SW7, Stratford-on-Avon, Normandy.

The Last of Spring 1929–1932. Rochester, The Eiffel, Monschau, Padstow, Denton (Kent), The Zugerberg (Switzerland), London W2.

The Purple Streak 1932–1933. Sarriá (Barcelona), the *Ponzano*, Wrotham, Madrid, Lisbon, Salperton (Glos.).

The Wild Hills 1933-1936. Salperton, London NW8, the Cotswolds, Cheltenham, Birmingham, the Scottish Highlands, Suffolk, Wales, Devon, Argentina.

The Happy Highways 1937-1938. Smarden (Kent), Kassel, travelling with a circus, travelling in a circus wagon in Europe, Belgium, Holland, Germany, Prague, Vienna, Budapest, Ljubljana, Milan, France, Kent.

The Sound of Revelry 1938-1939. London W1, Thomastown (Kilkenny), by coach to Naples, travelling with a circus Yorkshire, Alsace, Cologne, Paris; with circus again Sussex.

The Moon in My Pocket 1939-1940. Kent, Sussex, travelling with horse-drawn gypsy wagon, Pershore.

The Licentious Soldiery 1940-1943. Winchester, Chester, Glasgow, Barra, Durban, Mombasa, Zululand.

The Blood-Red Island 1942. Madagascar, Diego Suarez, Anivorano, Majunga, Tamatave, Tananarive.

The Gorgeous East 1943-1946. Bombay, Belgaum, Dehra Dun, Karachi, Poona, Saharanpur, Delhi, Kirkee.

The Dogs of Peace 1946-1950. London WC1, Scandinavia, the *Palomares* round Spain, Ashtead (Surrey). Marseilles, Madrid, Toledo, Paris.

The Life for Me 1950-1953. London WC1, Ticehurst, Normandy.

The Verdict of You All 1953. Ticehurst, Lewes, Wormwood Scrubs, London W2.

The Tangerine House 1953-1958. Cadiz, Tangier, Moroccan towns.

The Quest for Quixote (in US. *Through Spain with Don Quixote*) 1958. Tangier, Ciudad Real, Argamasilla de Alba, Torrenueva, El Toboso, Barcelona.

The Wintry Sea 1963. Tangier, Gibraltar, the *Trepća* to Savona,

Genoa, Naples, Catania (Sicily), Venice, Rijeka, Ljubljana, the *Ivan Mažuranić*, Tangier.

The Ghost of June 1967–1968. Tangier, London W2, Canterbury, Ham Common, Rye, Buscot, Underriver, Little Gaddesden, Cologne, Monschau, Paris, Gassin, St Tropez, Barcelona, Madrid, Almeria, Tangier.

Two books to follow and complete *The Sensual World:*

The Caves of Hercules 1958–1968. Tangier etc.

Not yet entitled 1968–1972. Normandy, London W2, Las Palmas, Gibraltar, Cyprus, Rome, Tunis, Dublin, Dun Laoghaire, Ceuta.

CHAPTER ONE
Welcome Home

[1]

EARLY in 1946 the words of that splendid old army song which I had many times shouted with my friends in its unbowdlerized version came true for me, for a troopship *was* leaving Bombay bound for old Blighty's shore, heavily laden with time-expired men. Whether or not they 'adored' the land for which they were bound, or would adore it much longer, was a matter for doubt.

What a troopship! Many times in my first three uncommissioned years in Combined Operations, entailing as they did whole months spent aboard ship, I had consoled myself for the cockroaches, the feeble beer, the cramped sleeping quarters by supposing that when I returned from the East I should be an officer and enjoy life on the upper deck, where in wardrooms or officers' bars whisky cost a few pence a measure. Small wonder that festive noises frequently reached us in our rat runs below. I remembered how one young Gunner, employed as a waiter in the officers' mess, had brought to our lower depths the printed menu in use that evening, and how a seasoned old sergeant had asked to see it. I remembered the expectorating disgust in his voice when he examined it. 'Christ!' he said. 'It's in fucking French!'

I went on board in Bombay not perhaps expecting to taste the luxury of a first-class passage home, for I knew that all troopships—by necessity I hope and not from some Whitehall whim—had become dry, but at least supposing I should have a reasonably comfortable passage to Liverpool. Even today I feel a faint flush of anger as I remember the conditions on this and other ships which brought our armies home from Burma and elsewhere, countries in which they had known abominable privations long after peace had come to Europe. Nothing which I, personally, had been forced to put up with in my six years in the army matched the squalor, discomforts and humiliations of that sweltering voyage, during which we as officers suffered rather more than the other ranks since they could sleep on the open decks and we were confined in a black hole of Calcutta. We were issued with hammocks, but there was so little room to hang them that they bumped against one another, and our food was garbage. The ship was not only dry but without any kind of canteen, recreation, reading matter or soft drinks. The officers and men she carried were not cheery old sweats accustomed to this sort of thing with whom one could perhaps have ridiculed and endured it, but disgruntled war-service men who growled and quarrelled among themselves dispiritedly. It was altogether a loathsome postscript to what had been six of the best years of my life, and seemed to have been contrived almost cynically to destroy any ideas we might have had that we were coming home to a land of plenty and pleasure.

Liverpool confirmed this as our train ran through its smoky suburbs, for we saw to our horror and embarrassment that from the back windows of little houses which overlooked the railway line had been hung soiled bunting and paper Union Jacks and WELCOME HOME signs, as though we were returning from the trenches of the First World War instead of being tired service men who had been forgotten in the East long after the only notable armistice, that with Germany, had been signed. The gesture was doubtless kindly meant, the sentimental inhabitants of those poor districts having realized that there were almost daily consignments of men on their way by train from Liverpool docks to Release Centres, but for me who could remember the Armistice of 1918 and the grey years which followed it for ex-service men, these poor little signs of welcome were almost unbearably foreboding and sad and seem to me now to have set the mood for the next five years of unhopeful peace.

They were, however, the only suggestions of welcome that we received or perhaps deserved and certainly the only ones of a public nature that any of us wanted. Privately we may have felt a touch of joy at being home and reunited with those we had not seen for three (or in my case four) years. We may have felt ourselves welcomed though it was usually with a reminder that those at home 'had been in the front line as much as we had', and perhaps more. So we were conducted through our Release Centres in a businesslike way, given our unwearable clothes and dispatched to our homes, free of the army at last.

In retrospect the twenty-four hours of my coming home to England seem like the first of Tom Brown's schooldays which, it may be remembered, occupies about a third of the book. Or did I spend a night at the Release Centre? I remember arriving in London at about four o'clock in the afternoon.

Then it was that the first extraordinary realization of what it would mean to me to return to civil life began. I had nowhere to go, no one to see with whom I was in touch, nothing of any point to do. It had not occurred to me to make any long-term preparations for this, nor had I realized that in those mad years of destruction and violent change almost everyone I knew had been uprooted. At first I tried a few phone calls to former friends but none of them could be found. My mother, already in her eighties, was living in the rooms she occupied until her death in her ninety-fifth year, and although she was waiting to see me could offer no accommodation. So there I was at a callbox with that shoddy bag of free clothing beside me, wearing my anomalous Captain's uniform, a very lost soldier. I wished I had never taken a commission so that I could have gone down to the Union Jack Club and been among the rowdy but understanding companions of my first years in the Army.

Finally, for want of any address I knew, I went to the offices of my then literary agents and began with their assistance to ring hotels in search of a room for the night. We tried over a dozen, from the Savoy to little bed-and-breakfast lodging houses round the main stations. Not one had a vacant room.

At last, when my agents had closed up and gone home, I thought of one man who surely would be still in London, for never in the sixty-odd years of his life did he spend more than a few hours away from it except for a year or two in the Army of the Rhine after the First World War. He may have gone with other Londoners to Brighton for a week-end but even this was rare and disturbed his habits uncomfortably. He at least would still be here, dodging round little drinking clubs and pubs at night, occupying a Covent Garden flat which he filled with paying guests since he did not like living alone, the very spirit of the frivolous, pleasure-loving and rather vacuous world of queer London, someone permanent around whom the meaningless lives revolved. So I telephoned Roy Hardy, whom I have described in earlier books in this series.

Yes, he still lived in Covent Garden and would be pleased to see me. His flat was fully occupied but he could, if I had nowhere better to go, give me a bed in his air-raid shelter which was in the cellars of the house. He was afraid it was a bit damp and had not been slept in for some time but there were blankets there. I gladly accepted and in due course went underground and slept the night away among a few friendly rats, being myself proof, by reason of recent experiences, against rheumatic fever.

So that was my home-coming. I deny emphatically that I felt or feel in retrospect any kind of self-pity about it. It was bizarre, even comic, rather than an occasion for maudlin sentiment. I had been phenomenally lucky throughout the war, enjoying the only holiday from writing I have ever known, delighting in a new kind of tourism and comradeship, savouring rich exploration in Madagascar, South Africa and India, given the double experience of life in the ranks for a happy three years and life as an officer for the last three, which were also the last of the British Raj in India, enjoying almost everything from my first recruitment to this first evening of so-called

Release. I realized it must all have a stop and I must begin to take up the White Man's Burden in a dull and ruined London along with the majority of my compatriots who instead of travelling and sightseeing had suffered in the desert, in Europe, in Burma or in the London blitz.

From my homecoming, leading down to that cellar, I realized without much apprehension that the good times were over, unless I could find ways of re-creating them, that henceforth my future, my ambitions, my pleasure in each day would depend on my own initiative and would no longer be handed to me on a silver WD platter.

[2]

My first necessity was to find a home, since like almost everyone else whose life had been interrupted by the war, I could think of nothing better to do than try to pick up the pieces. I wanted to start writing again, to live in London where I innocently believed that I could hold my own in that egomaniac society, the 'literary world'. It took about four years to disillusion me, and it is the story of those four years, full of comedy and colour, together with a few cynical recollections of the times we were passing through, that I wish to relate in this book. For me, for England, for the world at large they were, it will be remembered, very odd years indeed, 1946 to 1950, years in which there was a faster and more futile rate of change than perhaps ever before or since. We started trying to behave as we had done until 1939, since many of us still regarded 'before the war' as a halcyon time, though others cursed it as the epoch of hunger marches, unemployment and Munich. We started, as I say, trying to 'have a good time' as we believed we had done once. We found our flats and bought our cars undeterred by the shortage of domestic help and petrol, and gave our parties though there was not much gin, wore our civilian hats with an air and discussed books and plays over pub counters all as we had done so urgently in 1939. But before the end of those four years we had 'lost' as we put it, India, we had realized that once released into Europe neither the Americans nor the Russians were going quietly home to remain behind their boundaries but would be a permanent threat, in their different ways, to what was still called, without disrespect, the British way of life. We had begun to feel that rationing and public discipline were for ever and we had learned to live in a Welfare State. In my own life I had decided, once and for all, that I was not made for communal life, for a literary or any other society, that though I could live (sparsely but without actual want) by writing I should never be a successful, popular or well-known writer and certainly never a well-liked one. I should have formed a very large acquaintance among whom I should have made a few friends, but I could never be acceptable in—for instance—an old-established club or among a fashionable hostess's guests. Great trouble had been taken by many well-meaning people to make me a conventionally respected figure, but I had failed them all and at last I made for the comparative isolation of the countryside as a rabbit bolts for its burrow. But I would not have missed those four years for anything I can name, and the very recollection as I begin to write about them enlivens me. I was hopelessly at odds with the world about me and in spite of my naturally gregarious nature and the passionate love and hatred for *people* which confuse themselves in my Gemenian life, I see now that being so at odds was the state of mind which suited my temperament best.

[3]

First, as I say, a home, for I was no longer alone. I had adopted a young Indian whose skilful typing and even more astute accountancy—a prime need in my unbusinesslike life—would see me through the practical difficulties of authorship, as indeed they have done for thirty years down to the typing of this book. Joseph Susei Mari had already worked for my Field Security Section as a civilian clerk, for which I had obtained a special establishment from District HQ, and on his own account had learned shorthand and typing in preparation for my departure to England. I had refrained from adopting him legally, fearing lest this would make him liable for conscription in the United Kingdom, but had succeeded in obtaining a passage for him as a 'student' in which capacity he had travelled far more comfortably than I had. He was a Tamilian Catholic whose forbears had probably been converted by St Francis Xavier. He was now in rooms in Kent waiting to come to me when I had formed a household.

In the first days of searching for a home I realized that wartime changes had, above everything else, made England a country of 'Fuck you, Jack. I'm all right.' It was the only maxim that would long remain of the rich vocabulary of the Services and had become a guiding principle in urban life. People fought for living quarters in London as primeval men must have fought for the possession of the cosier caves and no holds were barred. Even fifteen years later prisons were stocked by screwy solicitors and land-agents who had been caught taking advantage of that war among the seekers for accommodation, while right down to the days of *Cathy Come Home* it continued among those who trusted in the promises made by local councils and such.

In 1946 it was at its most virulent and invidious in every class and at every price level. I can quote no statistics but I feel sure that a calculable number of murders were committed for the possession of living quarters and bitter quarrels broke out in hitherto civilized families and social groups.

I realized that I had come somewhat late into the conflict since the million or so who had left London for more protected regions during the war had now returned to occupy their former or other homes and the accumulated masses of wartime newly-weds were, understandably, clamouring rampantly for quarters. It was impossible, I was told again and again during my first days in London, to find any sort of home at less than prohibitive prices and almost impossible whatever one was prepared to pay. But one of the things one learns by the long experience of poverty, which is the professional writer's lot, is what *kind* of luck he may expect. God gives to everyone a measure of good fortune of some kind; it only remains to discover what it is, and what it is not. I knew, for instance, that I should never write a best-seller, never earn a literary award or one of those free holidays which are provided for writers, never be a rich or an important or widely respected man, never win even a minor prize in a lottery or sweepstake, never break the bank at Monte Carlo or even leave the casino richer than when I entered, never know security or permanence in life and never be one of those fortunate people whose very appearance of smiling benignance stamps them as free from the worries and frets of existence. But in other things, like finding a home or someone to do work for me that my full-time occupation does not allow me to do for myself, things like making friends or discovering cause for enjoyment in the least promising situations, things like finding old furniture, books or pictures where they are considered impossible to find, I am lucky, perhaps I should say supremely lucky, and in these my luck never fails, so that I have learned to count on it with childlike confidence.

It did not fail now. Within a week I had discovered a collection of very small rooms on the second and third floors of a half-ruined house in Covent Garden for which the owners had received a grant for repairs and for which, by some miraculous chance, they had not yet found a tenant. I seized them, decaying though they were, and sent for my furniture from Tenterden, where it had remained throughout the war in a little warehouse owned by a man with old-fashioned ideas about easy storage charges to those who had volunteered for army service. I might have lived for years in that poky if picturesque flat near the market if I had not been given there my first unpleasant taste of the new officialdom. I was informed that a housing committee of some sort, from (I think) Holborn Borough Council, wanted to inspect the rooms before final permission was given for their reconstruction, and would meet me, the prospective tenant, at a given time on the premises. I went to the flat and a troop of Councillors or Aldermen or what-have-you, led by a formidable woman named Mrs Jaeger or Jagger, filed up the stairs and looked at my pieces of furniture and pictures which seemed forlorn and misplaced in those dilapidated surroundings and asked me questions about my need to occupy the rooms as a separate flat. Was I married? What was my profession? Did I intend to use the rooms for any purpose other than private occupation?

I grew exasperated and asked them by what authority they were examining my possessions, a question they had no difficulty in answering with voluble quotations from bye-laws, housing regulations, rating authorizations or means tests, I forget which, after which they indignantly filed out again.

But by then I had discovered another home, no easier to occupy but far more congenial and less threatened by regulations, less inspected by housing officials and—once I had effected an entry—far more my own.

It was a 'flat on two floors' in Doughty Street, Bloomsbury, which a literary lawyer, a friend to many writers, had occupied with his wife and family for a number of years. With the end of an organization called the Freedom Association which he ran to the public benefit, Brendan Williams had decided to move to the country and, in spite of the wishes of the landlords—another organization called the Horace Plunkett Foundation—he decided to sublet the flat to me. It was a remarkable bargain because the pre-war rent, which could not legally be increased, was three pounds a week for its six rooms, three lofty and three, on the top floor, attic bedrooms, together with kitchen and bathroom.

The Horace Plunkett Foundation, occupying the lower floors,

was staffed by severe elderly ladies who filled the house with the incessant sound of their lavatory cistern refilling. They made the strongest objections to the subletting of their second- and third-floor flat to a bachelor with an Indian secretary and wanted to secure it for a puppeteer and his wife who had spent the war in America. There was consternation among them, consultation with lawyers, much telephoning and letter-writing, during which I quietly moved my furniture in before that of Brendan Williams had been fully moved out and thus presented them with a *fait accompli* which could not be gainsaid, unless by difficult litigation of doubtful outcome.

It was, I suppose, a fairly genteel version of the kind of grabbing and usurpation which was going on all over London wherever house-room became even momentarily vacant. It might have been called squatting or blockading, but the ladies of the Horace Plunkett Foundation, once they had recognized defeat, made no further effort to eject me and I remained in uninterrupted possession for four years, the envy of my friends. Certainly I would have preferred to live—as I had always done when in London—on the north side of the Park, in almost any region but Bloomsbury, and in almost any street but the early Victorian Doughty Street opposite to a house whose nameplate said it had been occupied by Charles Dickens so that it attracted sightseeing coach tours on summer evenings. Certainly I would have liked to return to the flat I had occupied before the war in Upper Berkeley Street, near the crowds and noise of Marble Arch, if that flat had not been destroyed by a bomb in 1940. But all in all, in spite of the greyness and hostility of Doughty Street, its associations with 'the Bloomsbury Set', the watchful ladies in the offices below my flat, the inaccessible coal cellar and the mustiness and dimness of the staircase, I agreed with my friends that I was lucky and having had the rooms redecorated with light and cheerful wallpapers made by Coles in Queen Anne patterns, I settled in to face what might be in the days ahead.

[4]

If I had made any real effort to return to the life I had so richly enjoyed before the war, my days would have been full of disillusionment. Fortunately I did not, but discovered the bitter humours, the lively compensations, the entertaining novelty of carving out a way to a new kind of hedonism. I would have been a 'nicer' but almost certainly a duller man if I had not inherited from my father the expressed belief that if you don't look after yourself no one will look after you. I do not *really* wish—though at times I think I do—to be an unworldly man, too occupied with ideas and philosophical considerations to be practical and a mite aggressive in my dealings with others, but I admit that this time there came out what is called 'the worst' in me as in all of us for whom life is a struggle not merely to survive but to enjoy surviving. I fought public authority, the insolence of office, the lassitude of others who accepted regimentation, the pretentiousness of doctrinaire politics, with every weapon in my private armoury. It was not Socialism in power that I hated, for (not from ingratitude, but with private apprehensions) I had wanted to see the end of Churchillism, but I resented the opinionated righteousness of the new rulers in their first years of victory. I remained as I had always been, a-political. The son of a blind blue-ribbon Conservative of Edwardian prejudices, I had liberated myself in thought to the point of anarchy and rebellion, but had never learned to love the only generally accepted alternative to my father's Conservatism, the all-embracing Left-Wing politics so popular among my fellow-writers both before the war and now. These politics awoke in me both the prejudices of my bourgeois class origins and at the other extreme, the contempt engendered by what I considered my far more seditious will to rebel. In this, as in so much else, I realized my isolation and the conflicts it would bring me. When you cannot feel any loyalty even to something as popular as the Left Wing, or as eccentric and old-fashioned as the Right, you are indeed alone. And when I found myself resenting every display of petty authority which the people about me had learned by custom to accept I ran into some infuriating situations.

Perhaps it came from service life in which everyone was someone else's superior, but there was noticeably at that time the most insulting officiousness. 'You insolent fellow!' my father would have said if he had lived to suffer from it, but it would be because the 'fellow' had been 'insolent' to *him* and not out of indignation at the general overbearing manner which sent the weakest to the wall. Although I felt I could well take care of myself, I was angry because I saw the feelings of gentle people, of timorous and naturally submissive people being trampled on by loud-mouthed bullies, frequently in uniform. It was a feature, and a very unpleasant feature, of London at that time and may have been understandable because of the continuance of shortages, the miseries of the immediate past or popular exasperation after a long war. For the only time I can remember the Londoner, who has his own cheerful good manners, became surly and rude and every jack-in-office a petty tyrant. It did not last, in the general public, but among policemen, public transport officials, shop stewards, members of the countless committees which rule our lives, some of its arrogance has persisted to this day.

I remember one evening, soon after I had moved into 10 Doughty Street, going to a cinema in Leicester Square and purchasing two tickets for the next performance. There was a quarter of an hour to pass and I suggested to the friend who was with me that we should go to a neighbouring pub for a drink. To my amazement the commissionaire barred our way.

'You can't leave the cinema,' he said.

'I what?'

'You can't leave the cinema. Not now you've booked seats.'

I was so dumbfounded that I said nothing but avoided his restraining arms and walked out.

'You'll get into trouble,' he called after me. 'I shall tell the manager!'

And by God he did, so that a flustered-looking man in a dinner-jacket awaited me in the foyer on my return. He tried to say something about the rules and threatened feebly to prevent my entering. Ignoring this I walked in and found my seat. But what staggered me was the attitude of the friend accompanying me.

'You shouldn't have gone out,' he said, and finally, in summary, '*It's not allowed.*' A trivial incident but one which, if ever there was one, was a straw in the wind.

There were others. A cyclist who stood shouting in front of my car in a traffic jam, because he claimed that I had 'cut him off', a bus conductor who became abusive because I had no change smaller than a pound note, and more than one policeman full of truculent authority, though to be just the poor old flatty on his beat, as opposed to the CID, is not an aggressive fellow. All these might have happened at any time in any capital city, but it was more than a coincidence that they happened to me in that particular epoch in London. With the outbreak of peace there was lost, for a time, much of the crude but amiable courtesy of the Cockney and the ladies and gentlemen of Kensington, that mythical abode of *nice* people, screeched and argued with one another in the streets.

[5]

I soon found other unfortunate changes and horrors which, because they had developed slowly over the years of my absence, and had been explained away and excused by characters in government like Lord Woolton (an arch-apologist for shortages), were taken for granted by the people about me but to me seemed cataclysmic in their significance. Many of them are forgotten now, for we put out of mind the annoyances of the past, but let us never forget what we endured in the years immediately after the war while most others countries in Western Europe and the Americas were thriving.

I remember hearing of restaurants where good and plentiful food was miraculously obtainable at not too outrageous prices, only to find crowded eating-houses where horsemeat, disguised as fillet steak, was condescendingly served by insolent Cypriots. I remember the power shortage of 1946–1947, not for any privation it caused me because I was in a district of no cuts, but for the sense of guilt and conviction of selfishness it induced. I remember the shifts, some of them dishonest and anti-social, which I and others were put to by the system in force of petrol rationing, and how it actually sent Ivor Novello to Wormwood Scrubs. 'Can you let me have any petrol coupons? Or clothes coupons? I can offer some coupons for this or that in exchange,' we told our friends, when we could not obtain what we needed on the black market.

'Ways round' could nearly always be found. As a writer needing 'copy' I was able to travel abroad, as a dealer in books and pictures I obtained extra petrol coupons, while like almost every other knowledgeable inhabitant of a particular district I soon found occasional sources for clothes, meat and groceries, and never went short of cigarettes. Except during my first week or two in civil life when I stayed in a Blackheath hotel I never found a pub closed for lack of supplies. So it was not the *shortages* which angered me, for these could nearly always be remedied. It was the time I wasted and the feeling that I was no better than a spiv—that significant contemporary word. It was also the knowledge gained from a crossing of the channel in 1947 that no such shortages were known in France, a country recently enemy-occupied.

[6]

The Government, so long synonymous with Churchill since behind his voluminous personality its various members had seemed to remain concealed, became a number of individuals rousing nearly as much public detestation as Baldwin had done in his worst days. For me their very faces roused derision, cocky little Morrison apparently believing that what we wanted was not the re-building of ruined London but the raising of ridiculous erections for an ill-timed Festival of Britain. Clumsy Ernest Bevin saying that he wanted to see a free Europe in which we could cross frontiers without difficulty and then making it impossible by a niggardly travel allowance, plausible Aneurin Bevan whose personal charm, vouched for by all who knew him, seemed to me suspect, and Stafford Cripps whose lack of it was painfully evident. I respected Attlee because without prolonged and fruitless palaver he cut short the anomalous anachronism of the British Raj in India. But those years, under that government, made me detest not only politics, as I had long done, but politicians as I do to this day, so that my antipathy wavers between Heath with his plummy voice and self-satisfied manner and Wilson with his air of being confident that he is clever enough to argue the hind leg off the British public. For once I was not alone in that detestation. Not only the deprived middle classes who had wanted Churchill but the very people who had voted Labour blamed all their personal troubles on the men they had elected. They paid small attention to such things as our precarious balance of payments, or the rising expenses of a visionary welfare state subsidized from taxation, but believed—what was probably the case—that it was sheer ineptitude which made the Government deny them the sweets of victory.

So it was a shabby, disgruntled, impoverished society, alive with deserters, small-time criminals and black marketeers, which moved among the bombed houses and burnt-out buildings of London in which I settled that spring of 1946, and determined to write again as never before, to make new friends and find new adventures, in a word to enjoy without doting selfishness the life which God in his generosity had given me.

CHAPTER TWO
Litigation and Reviewing

[1]

So I settled into that flat—Regency or early Victorian? The exact date of construction was not known but it had very little remnant of grace from the Georgian architecture of an earlier date. On the lower of my two floors which had tall ceilings I made a living-room looking out on to the identical houses across the street, a study looking over to the Bloomsbury roofs at the back, and a little office for Joseph. Telephone, electricity, gas, an infallible hot-water system, a frigidaire, basic floor covering of dark brown linoleum everywhere—it had the amenities considered necessary for convenient living. All it lacked was the lightsome cheeriness of that low-ceilinged flat in Upper Berkeley Street which I had left on the outbreak of war. It was *older* and more dignified, of course, without being truly in period, but then I was older myself and no longer so interested in filling my severely decorated rooms with the thieving riff-raff I had met in the Edgware Road. I was, I assured myself, a seriously-minded writer anxious to rebuild what reputation I had before the war, a householder with the responsibility of a large rather gloomy home in a building dedicated to work, with weekly payments to find for a secretary and a housekeeper, and for a time I made a serious but fore-doomed attempt to live in character.

My first conflict—one deliberately entered upon—was a piece of litigation against the bugbear of my pre-war writing life, the publisher Walter Hutchinson. He it was who in my first years as a very young novelist had taken advantage of a complaint of libel directed against me by a Swiss schoolmaster, and keeping me tied by contract to his firm had required that I should write during one incredible period no less than *five* novels in twelve months for the reward of sixteen pounds a month, and when I predictably failed to produce more than two novels in a year he had added the amount paid to me on the remaining three to my total debt to his firm, thus holding me at the oar of his galley till I had found strength to revolt.

When I came out of the army I still owed one novel under this contract, and I delivered a satirical book called *Octopus* which pleased his staff. (He never read the books he published —there was in fact a strong rumour that he could not read at all except the racing news.) But during leaves in India in the last two years I had finished another cheerful somewhat picaresque novel called *Ladies Gay* which my agents had sold to Macdonalds. Now I found that Hutchinson, with deliberate malice, it seemed to me, had delayed publication of his novel to bring it out just a fortnight before the other.

Not many people would enter into litigation with the gusto I showed to solicitors and to a barrister named Lawton who had unwillingly agreed to be Counsel for me in a case in which the outcome was so dubious. But primed with the indignation I felt from all I had suffered from Walter Hutchinson in the nine years of my writing career before the war I strained to get at his throat and eventually persuaded Lawton that we should sue for breach of contract, a plea based on the firm's failure to publish, as they had contracted to do, within six months of my delivery of the manuscript.

It was a headstrong and youthful thing to do but I was both headstrong and in such matters inexperienced. Nowadays I should avoid litigation at any cost short of the loss of self-respect but then it seemed a light-hearted adventure and one which would give me my revenge on a pig-headed totally insensitive extortioner but for whom, I believed, I might have written good novels. I entered into conferences with Counsel, obtained witnesses and prepared my own testimony as though the whole thing was a schoolboy play in which I had been picked for the part of Stalky. Neither before nor after that time have I shown myself to be litigious but then I expected to romp through the Chancery Court to the bafflement of Hutchinson himself and his minions.

[2]

It was while I was preparing for the case against Walter Hutchinson that I met, for the first time since 1932, a man who had influenced my writing life considerably, the late John Collings Squire, Jack Squire of the *London Mercury*, of the Invalids Cricket Club, Jack Squire the poet, as he would wish and deserves to be called. He offered to give evidence on my behalf—quite what evidence was not much discussed—but evidence which in the days of Squire's prime would have swayed any Court concerned with a matter of writing and publishing.

His story deserves re-telling not as I shall tell it here in a few inadequate paragraphs but from a long-standing intimacy with the subject to which Squire's excellent biographer Patrick Howarth* does not pretend. It is not a Boswell that Squire's memory needs but a Lytton Strachey, a bitchy, percipient, appreciative, ruthless writer who would realize both the achievement and pathos of his scarred life, as Howarth does, but portray him in its various contrasting stages as well. And he would be worth it. His image was muddied during his later years, and his service to the literature of our time was overridden by the quick changes in poetic fashion in the thirties, the swing of adulation to Eliot not merely as a poet but as an arbiter, with his pretentious *Criterion*. Jack Squire, who had been an oversocial drinker since his young manhood, became—there was no concealing it—a drunk, but even in his worst years he was

* Patrick Howarth *Squire: Most Generous of Men.* 1963.

more of a talkative and irresponsible drunk than a lugubrious alcoholic given to lonely inebriation. He could keep his end up in conversation, in wit and in anecdote to the end. He may have been, in the words of a popular song, a headache to a great many people, but he never was a bore.

I had known him since my teens when he wrote encouraging letters about poetry I had sent him and invited me, as he did so many of the hopeful embryo writers of that time, to the warehouse-like office of the *London Mercury* in Poppins Court where he lectured me on the need to read W. H. Hudson before leaving for South America. Eventually, after my fifth or sixth attempt to be included among the young poets he attracted, he accepted a poem of mine for the *Mercury*. He remained a godfatherly friend through all my first years of hard work, advising, introducing, planning till I could more or less stand on my own feet. He had an air of great enthusiasm in all matters literary and more friendships than he had time to maintain, though he gave the best part of his life to the attempt. He was full of contradictions—he had started public life as a Socialist and clung to the label long after the Old School (he was at Blundell's, Tiverton) and his passionate devotion to cricket which he played poorly, and his naturally upper-middle-class prejudices, had superseded his first ideals. But he was, as his biographer maintains, the most generous of men, generous not only to the young and ambitious whose characters marched with his own but to the elderly failures of his profession, generous with time (the noblest form of generosity), with interest in even the alien pursuits of his friends, generous with encouragement, criticism, good talk and entertainment.

In 1947 his only points of contact with reality were his weekly articles for the *Illustrated London News* and his occasional appearances on the cricket field. He was a white-haired London nomad who could not control the shaking of his hands or his wayward walk. He wore anything he could find and I once drove him down to West Wickham to play for his cricket team, the Invalids, wearing a pyjama jacket, a pair of very yellow flannel trousers and patent leather shoes. Yet that was a glorious occasion on which nobody, host, opponents or fellow-Invalids, appeared to notice anything odd in his appearance.

It was also for me the beginning of a friendship which has lasted to this day with Alec Waugh, who had played for the Invalids for twenty-five years. That afternoon there was a notable batting partnership lasting nearly an hour between Alec and his young son, then still at Sherborne. This gave Squire such obvious pleasure that his humorous kindly face and short-sighted eyes behind thick glasses twinkled and creased with happiness. We went later to a Chelsea pub in which Jack was known to the customers in the public bar as 'Sir John', this being pronounced without sarcastic intent, patronage or undue respect but simply as the name which was rightfully and naturally his, however discordant it might seem with the surroundings. He talked without ever losing either his temper or his interest in whatever topic occurred and his virile, curiously cultured voice never failed to hold his hearers' attention.

When my lawsuit with Hutchinson was to be heard in the Chancery Court I felt a certain anxiety about Jack. Would he remember to appear at all? If so, in what garb and state of insobriety? I need not have worried. He had asked me for ten pounds to cover his expenses and evidently felt this bound him in honour to give evidence. He appeared punctually in the remains of a formal suit, and although he was never called it was not for any reason connected with himself.

For some years I did not see much of Jack. He had an embarrassing habit of saying quite erroneously to people in front of me that he had known me, and predicted a literary future for me, when I was still a boy at Tonbridge. Moreover he was often considered unpresentable by self-righteous friends who had not known him in the glorious days of his appearances in *Georgian Poetry*, his literary editorship of the *New Statesman*, his founding and editorship of the *London Mercury*, his weekly articles in the *Observer*, his *Selections from Modern Poets*, and his immense popularity and championship of every cause which seemed in his lively mind defensible. '*Pas sortable*', one of them said, truthfully enough but rather meanly. There were splendid qualities in Jack even in his decline, and I am glad to remember that in 1953, five years before his death, I went by invitation —to which the proviso, 'bring a bottle of something' was added—to see him at Bassett's Mill, Chiddingstone Heath, in Kent where he was looked after in rustic comfort by Bertha Usborne. He was still a literary adviser to Macmillans, who were then publishing my novels, and he had something not very useful to say about one of them. He was by then patriarchal in appearance with a white beard, and he persisted in all his kindly-meant errors of fact, saying that I had contributed to the *London Mercury* while still a boy at Tonbridge. We made a plan, never alas realized, to run down to Horsham and visit Hilaire Belloc, then eighty-three years old, a man of heroic stature in my eyes, whom I had not seen since the war.

'We must take him some wine,' said Jack and incredibly added that Belloc now only cared for white port. Belloc died a month or two later, so that the journey with its improbable offering was never made, but Jack himself lived past his seventieth birthday, celebrated by a party of his friends at the Garrick Club, and passed a bedridden but clear-minded year before his death at the end of 1958 in his seventy-fifth year. From Tangier, to which I had by then emigrated, I mourned him, as I had enjoyed his friendship, alone. I had never been one of the well-defined collections of his friends, neither a Mercurian nor an Invalid, neither a member of the Squirarchy in the 1920s nor one of those who felt they should avoid Jack in the days of his eclipse. But I can still repeat much of his poetry and parodies by heart and still rejoice in my good fortune in having known the man.

[3]

I lost the lawsuit against Hutchinson, of course, and dare say I deserved to do so for such foolhardiness and thirst for revenge. Hutchinson had as Counsel a KC of some considerable reputation at that time, the late Sir Valentine Holmes, and the judge, whose name I forget though his weak features decorated by his wig are still vivid to me, seemed so impressed by Holmes that the thing became a sort of petting party between the two of them.

'If you're going to say so-and-so, Mr Lawton,' the Judge warned my Counsel, 'Sir Valentine will have something to say about that. Won't you, Sir Valentine?'

'I shall indeed, M'lord,' said the eminent barrister dutifully, and so the thing went on. All right, so I *had* brought an action which depended on the letter rather than the spirit of the law, but Hutchinson *had* ignored his contract to publish within so many months—I forget whether it was six or twelve, but in any case he was well over it, and he *had* planned to ditch my first book with another publisher. Costs were given to Hutchinson but his claim, based on his KC's fee, was so reduced by the costing master that it did not mean a very serious loss to me, and taught me a lesson which I should have learned in childhood, to keep away from law courts at almost any price. Not long afterwards Hutchinson committed suicide and the firm that now bears his name has no connection with his dubious methods and reputation, having been raised anew out of the ruins that he left.

But my unsuccessful Action was not all loss. Surely everyone at some point in his adult life should have at least one experience of the theatrical mummery of the Law, the grotesque drag which its practicants wear to distinguish them from outsiders to their profession (as they consider all the rest of the world), the invidiousness and common-room humour in their Chambers, their addictive gambling at the expense of laymen. Lawyers as

I know them away from the Courts are more often than not characters of considerable charm, keeping alive in a drab age the arts and graces of life, collectors, connoisseurs, conversationalists and men of no less integrity than their fellows. They are certainly not martyrs or fanatics trying to serve a Cause—they give the impression of having too much commonsense for that. But their councils and temples should be carefully avoided by those who seek peace of mind, for many a pleasant life has been ruined by litigation, and across the years I sympathetically remember a little house in Eastbourne which had been plastered from roof to ground with immense placards proclaiming the caveat *Beware of Lawyers* 'Some crank,' my father remarked when he saw it and he was doubtless right, but that disgruntled house-owner, carrying on his one-man war against a profession, still wakes an echo of sympathy in me.

[4]

All this wasted a great deal of time, and I became very much aware of the necessity to get down to work and began the novel which of all my books earned me most credit though not, as usual, most cash. This was *Wilkie*, the story of a retired Colonel of the Indian Army, a subject curiously popular with English novelists from Thackeray onwards, but one which I believed I could treat in a new, cruelly contemporary manner.

At the same time I was appointed, in succession, to L. P. Hartley who was doubtless tired of the job, book critic to the weekly illustrated *Sketch*, at that time a flourishing member of the Illustrated Newspaper group, *The Tatler*, the *Illustrated Sporting and Dramatic* and the rest. Today they have been reduced by the competition of television and illustrated supplements to one heroic survivor, *The Illustrated London News*, a weekly in which, as a preparatory schoolboy, I had studied pictures of the Balkan War.

The delightful thing about the *Sketch* was not the money I earned from it, for if it had not been for the sale of review copies this would have been almost (though never quite) negligible, but the freedom it gave me under two editorships to choose the books I wrote about and deal with them in complete liberty, sometimes verging on licence. There was not space for deeply-considered or wordy criticism and I never attempted it.

Looking over those pages which appeared every fortnight for six years, I am confronted with proof of what a painfully barren period that was for English fiction. Few names emerged which still mean anything to readers, and there are scores and scores of first novels which were issued with bright promise by their publishers and were never succeeded by a second. There were attempts by powerful firms to 'launch' new names to awe us, but most of them have fallen in the dust.

I decided at once that I would do all I could to keep alive the reputations of those writers who had known some eminence or success before the war and now seemed to be falling into danger of obliteration. Some of these were my contemporaries or juniors, some of an older generation, some had been best-sellers and some wrote greatly respected but uncommercial books. They were not all of them writers whose achievements I passionately admired, but they were professionals and they needed the encouragement of an enthusiast in even the comparatively obscure book-page of the *Sketch*.

Looking through a collection of those reviews I think that it comprises almost a complete fiction catalogue for the years 1946–52, and there may be some interest in one man's view of this.

I see now that I raised a cheer for my predecessor, L. P. Hartley, whose *Eustace and Hilda* came out in 1947, 'his prose rises to an almost epic pitch', and several cheers for Gerald Kersh, who published a number of novels in that and the succeeding years, all of which I admired. But I could not rise to Charles Morgan whose work I thought was 'distinguished, skilled and humourless' and who was a 'master of phraseology rather than of prose'. I went to town on my old friend Rhys Davies: 'With full responsibility for the word I must call this (*The Dark Daughters*) a great novel.' Of Mollie Panter-Downes, whom I remembered as a child prodigy when she wrote *The Shoreless Sea* at the age of sixteen, I said that *One Fine Day*, a racy and delightful book, had 'a quality rare in modern novels, a kind of magnetism which makes one look forward to the time when one will have forgotten its details sufficiently to want to read it again'.

Obviously I joined the chorus of praise for the novels of Evelyn Waugh and Graham Greene, for they seemed about the only serious hope we had of finding something durable in our transient age, but also I went for Claude Houghton in a big way, a novelist of very peculiar and individual achievement. In one number in 1948 I reviewed H. E. Bates, R. C. Sherriff and Taylor Caldwell who had, perhaps, all been overpraised in various ways, and a few weeks later wrote up Ethel Mannin and Neil M. Gunn, and called *Storm and Echo*, a new book by Frederic Prokosch (another infant prodigy of pre-war), 'a magnificent tour-de-force'. In the next year a new book by Magdalen King-Hall, another writer established before the war, *Tea at Crumbo Castle* seemed to me very good indeed. I felt I came near to making a discovery in John Lodwick's early book, *Peal of Ordnance*, but I had known the work of Storm Jameson, John Pudney and Georgette Heyer before the war and was happy to greet it now. A new name to me (in May 1948) was Francis King whose *Never Again* I heartily recommended, while I gave a loud welcome to Jocelyn Brooke. I thought Lawrence Durrell in his first unpseudonymous novel *Cefalu* 'clever—much too clever to be a good novelist or even, I cannot help thinking a very good writer', an opinion I in no way forswear. I said Olivia Manning could write as few novelists can, thought that *William Medium* by Edward Hyams 'did not quite come off' and praised those long-established writers

G. B. Stern (*No Son of Mine*), Gilbert Frankau (*Michael's Wife*) and Howard Spring (*There is No Armour*).

But I really went to town on two even longer and perhaps more deservedly established writers, Oliver Onions and Gerald Bullett. The former in his last years became a much admired friend, and it remains incredible to me that his qualities as a writer were not more widely recognized. The same was true of Liam O'Flaherty, who published a book of short stories in 1948, *Two Lovely Beasts*, though O'Flaherty had had his moment in the sun at the time he wrote *The Informer*. I rather patronizingly said of Saul Bellow that he had 'a certain rather fickle talent and will almost certainly write good books' and I did not think much of the American author of *The Lost Week-End*, Charles Jackson, whose second novel, a timorous study of homosexuality, was published in 1948 as *The Fall of Valour*.

A novelist who had published his first work in the *New Coterie* and his first novel in the same year as mine was sure of a space on my page, and James Hanley got it for *Emily*, 'a fine and distinguished piece of work—as good as anything the author has done', while I did not forget A. J. Cronin or C. S. Forester, both at this particular time rather obscure. But I must have been relieved, I think, to leave all these for a loud welcome to bright new names, like Truman Capote whose *Other Voices, Other Rooms* appeared at this time and Angus Wilson whose *The Wrong Set*, followed by *Such Darling Dodos*, were the foundations of his considerable reputation today.

I could be bitchy, too, especially to deafeningly praised writers whom I thought second-rate. I quote verbatim from my review of *Sons of Noah* by Negley Farson.

> I started this novel without any marked optimism, for I was not an admirer of his *Way of a Transgressor* and remember a trivial and misleading book which Mr Farson wrote about South America. My hopes rose when I thought that it was to be about an isolated community living by the salt marshes of the New Jersey coast, the

fishermen of a place called Mollusc, where a small, independent oyster fleet gave the people their only means of support and occasionally sent typhus epidemics across the States. This seemed a promising background, and there soon appeared a particularly luscious heroine with 'wide deep eyes, full lips' and a 'sun-burned high-cheek-boned face', 'the sort of face that made you wonder what the world will do to its owner'. Like the narrator, I found it 'disturbing to look at her', but when the same narrator reflected that 'for a long time her straining youth was going to trouble her more than it would anyone else', I was not so sure. It might trouble the reader a good deal, too, I thought, and sure enough it did. The book soon ceases to deal with the community at Mollusc. The fishermen appear to have been introduced as picturesque extras in the opening scene, and soon we're off on a long tortuous story of a young doctor who is in love with the girl but believes her to be his half-sister, and so spends all his time in a small yacht alone with a Negro crew of one. There are some wholly irrelevant but far more entertaining 'socialite' drunks and dyspeptics, and quite a lot of ground is covered in various parts of America before there is an overdue happy ending. But there is one final piece of whimsy which more difficult to swallow. The narrator gives the heroine a copy of *Kim*. 'And Kim eventually did find the river where the arrow fell. It was the Patuxent.'

Also a similar piece about a book named *Kenny* by a similar writer, Louis Bromfield:

Things, alas, are not always what they seem, and books sometimes have entrails which belie their outward and physical appearances. A first glance at this one would lead one to suppose that it was a new novel by Mr Louis Bromfield and concerned a character whose name gave it its title. In fact, it consists of two long short stories of approximately equal length, and a shorter one. The title-piece is a sentimental trifle about an Ohio waif on a farm, with a disconcerting habit of disappearing at night to sleep in the woods, particularly when there was a full moon. However, he had 'the rippling muscles, the dark-tanned skin and the catlike grace—indeed, all the things which made other men seem somehow mis-shapen and awkward', and which caused the schoolgirls to 'gather in little groups, watching him, talking about him and giggling'. He had, in fact, 'a strange, heady effect upon the girls and even upon older women', so that it was just as well, perhaps, that there was a 'curious cleanness and chasteness' about him. The war saw Kenny in the Marines, for that corps is to American novelists what the Commandos are to ours—the almost inevitable home for hero and hard case alike. He was made a Top Sergeant 'because other men always loved and respected him. Where women fell in love with him, men admired him.' There was the usual Tennessee buddy called Buck and a photograph of them both in which Kenny was seen to have 'lost none of the wild faun-like appearance'. He was killed during an island engagement with the Japanese, and he and his dog 'just went up to Heaven in a burst of fire'. When Buck returned to the farm where Kenny had worked, Kenny's widow felt as if Kenny had sent him back to take care of her. She married Buck, and when their first baby was born he resembled neither of them, because 'Kenny—or what was the essence of Kenny—had managed to come back'.

But at about that same time I became excited, with good cause, over the first of Henry Cecil's books about the law and lawyers which have since achieved great popularity. It was called *Full Circle* and I wrote:

A reviewer's hopes of finding that he has made a 'discovery' are small nowadays, with vigilant book societies, clubs and leagues on every hand, and a good many periodicals regularly and seriously considering new books. Long before this is published, I feel sure, Mr Cecil will have been acclaimed by others as a highly interesting newcomer. All the same, I should like to record my own personal excitement as I first began to read him. There has been nothing in this particular vein one-half so good since Saki was alive.

Throughout the whole period in which I reviewed for the *Sketch* there were certain writers of whom I knew nothing personally but who had roused my enthusiasm and kept me interested in everything they did. Of these William Sansom was one. He was not as young as I thought he was, but he had been unknown till after the war and his short stories immediately took my breath away. Gwyn Jones was another such writer and Denton Welch, who died during this period, was another. New for the most part to me, though to no one else who cared for good writing, was the work of William Plomer of whom I wrote, 'The only regret one can feel about Mr Plomer's work is that there is not more of it.'

Among crime writers I championed those I thought most intelligent, which did not include Dorothy L. Sayers or such, and argued for Roy Vickers, Nicholas Blake and Michael Innes, and I paid my tribute to that indefatigable old literary pro, Agatha Christie.

I wrote of *Arras of Youth* by Oliver Onions that 'this is a book to make most of us who try to write novels feel that we should have taken up brick-laying'. But did I really say of Nigel Balchin's *A Sort of Traitor* that 'it is all rather like a good film—and no doubt it will make one'? Or of John Mortimer's *Rumming Park* that the whole story is milk-and-Waughter? Or of George Orwell's *Nineteen Eighty-Four* that its final irony is that 'if it is widely read enough it may never happen'? I certainly wrote and still stand by my opinion of Osbert Sitwell's *Laughter in the Next Room*:

> I seem to be almost alone among reviewers in not being moved to ecstasy by this new volume of Sir Osbert

Sitwell's autobiography, but I recommend it only to those who are already familiar with the earlier books in this series, and wish to hear more of the people described in them. Starting the story here I find its trivial content, overweighted by its grandiose Victorian prose and the author's assumption that his reader is already 'in the know' with him about his comic servants and eccentric relatives, more than a little irritating.

I was disappointed, as befitted a lifelong advocate of Sinclair Lewis as perhaps the foremost American novelist of the century (despite later modes and reputations), with his last novel *The God-Seeker* (1949) and I evidently ran against opinion at that time in saying of Nancy Mitford's *Love in a Cold Climate*, 'This novel is also meant to be funny but succeeds only in patches, leaving large and desolate areas for the reader to tramp across ... I doubt whether many readers will fall into the uproarious convulsions promised in the blurb.' I must have been getting my own back on John Brophy when I quoted from his *Julian's Way*: ' "Sometimes," says Margit, "I think I am the only person in the world who understood Sir John." "And sometimes," I added, "I think she is right." Certainly I did not and I found myself wondering whether the author did.'

I highly approved, I was glad to remember when he became my friend later, of Paul Bowles's *The Sheltering Sky*, and paid tribute to the professionalism and industry of C. P. Snow's novels and of Margaret Steen's *Twilight of the Floods*, Daphne du Maurier's *The Parasites*, and with less interest to Upton Sinclair's *One Clear Call*. I was never lost in wonderment at the genius of Joyce Cary and said of his new novel, *A Fearful Joy*, that it 'might have been dictated on a fast journey and be intended for the entertainment of passengers on an airliner. It has an affectation of breathless speed, as though the author heard a voice telling him all the time to come along and not waste time on details. A paragraph may dispose of a couple of lives, a love-story and a career. But this does not represent a genuine economy; it is a kind of condensation which results in vertigo rather than attentiveness from the reader.' But I remember the very day on which I read a novel by Richard Llewellyn, whose *How Green Was My Valley* I had missed. The novel was *A Few Flowers for Shiner*, and I said Llewellyn 'had done that well-nigh impossible thing—depicted the comradeship of life in the Services without a hint of the mawkish or embarrassing'. I wrote of Rex Warner's *Men of Stone* that 'his cold lucid prose, his starkly silhouetted narrative recall Swift or at moments Defoe', and was equally enthusiastic about P. H. Newby's *The Young May Moon*.

When Sheila Kaye-Smith, whose work and personality I had greatly admired for twenty years, produced a new novel, *Treasures of the Snow*, I did my best to feel the old enthusiasm but without more than partial success, and when the same happened in the case of James Branch Cabell I made the same effort, and once again the same for Rose Macaulay's *The World My Wilderness*. But how I longed, in those years, to find something in fiction both new and worthwhile and how I was disappointed. I could not even feel excited about Doris Lessing, who emerged at that time with *The Grass is Singing*, though I admitted that it had 'the blessed stamp of authenticity'.

Why I was so unkind to Violet Trefusis that she wrote me sixteen pages in expostulation I cannot now remember, nor why I called Nevil Shute's *A Town Like Alice* 'a slipshod ill-constructed novel which seems to have been cobbled together from two distinct stories', but Shute was one of those novelists who seemed to write books pre-destined for a facile popularity. Frank Tilsley was a more worthwhile proposition and I thought *The Jungle of Your Heart* 'a conscientious, honest tale with motives under the microscope and everyone treated with justice'.

I found little merit in Gore Vidal, 'who as a writer seems to live, like Henry I, under an oath never to smile again' and 'just as in *The City and the Pillar* turns his golden material to lead'. He has made a considerable reputation since then and as I have failed to follow it I do not know how my predictions worked out. Even less charitably I said of a sentimental novel called *Geordie*, 'to me, I must own, the whole thing seems conceived and written as a powerful emetic'. But I liked Evelyn Waugh's novel *Helena*, 'the legend of St Helena recounted with all the liveliness and insouciance that was once dedicated to Agatha Runcible'.

I was getting into my stride at the end of 1950 and deciding that George Barker's *The Dead Seagull* 'was a worthwhile experiment which might prove a successful one' and that Angela Thirkell's books were 'mild pleasant family chronicles, never very funny or very tragic, about people who are not very good or bad, happy or unhappy'. It is a pity that no novel from Colin McInnes appeared in those years to remedy the massive mediocrity of his mother's work, which I supposed matched that of Mazo de la Roche, though I have never been able quite to finish one of their books.

I put my shirt on Warren Tute and his novels of naval life called *The Felthams* and *Gentlemen in Pink Uniform*, but such is my ignorance of fiction since the *Sketch* died that I do not know whether he followed them up. I found a very sincere book appearing from James Courage, a New Zealander who long ago had been struggling with his first novel in a bungalow I rented in Cornwall. He died shortly afterwards—the loss of a delicate talent.

I was kept occupied by a more or less distinguished contemporary company without surprises—Phyllis Bottome, Nigel Balchin, Enid Bagnold, H. E. Bates, Elizabeth Taylor and others, whose books were published regularly during those years.

I liked the first of Anthony Powell's series *A Question of Upbringing* but did not see (who could?) what was to come of it. 'My only moment of foreboding was when I read in the blurb the words "and subsequent volumes". A series of sequels would, I feel, be too much of what is certainly a good thing.'

Of I. Compton-Burnett, not yet a fashionable craze, I wrote, 'Miss Compton-Burnett is one of those authors who divide most of us sharply into sheep and goats—the fans who tell you, suppressing their retrospective mirth and pleasure, that there is nothing quite like her work, that she is the wittiest and most profound of novelists, and on the other hand that yawning company of people who say that they simply do not understand what it's all about. I find myself, unfortunately, unable to join whole-heartedly either faction,' and adopted much the same non-committal attitude to J. B. Priestley's novel *Festival at Farbridge*. There were other voices which recalled past enthusiasms at about that time, late-flowering novels from Eden Philpotts, Patrick Hamilton, Howard Spring, Gerald Bullett and Wyndham Lewis, none of them of much importance.

Then there was a noisy new arrival, *The Cruel Sea* by Nicholas Montserrat. There was so much anticipatory fuss and promise worked up about this novel that I was prejudiced before I read it, and when the publishers invited all the newspaper critics of the time to a party on a Thames steamer for its publication day, I sulked and refused to go. So it was necessary for me to read the book carefully and consider what I could justly say about it. I reviewed it among 'Books in Brief'. 'A good book on a subject which deserves a great one,' I summarized and do not regret that opinion. Other names were attracting attention—Louis Auchinloss whom I compared to 'that good forgotten novelist Edith Wharton', Robin Maugham with whom a long and intimate friendship bars me from competently judging his work, Olivia Manning whose *School for Love* I called one of the 'gayest and most readable novels to be published since the war', the ghost-story writer H. P. Lovecraft, Pamela Hansford Johnson, Gwyn Thomas, Paul Bowles and Henry Treece, whose novel of Roman Britain, *The Dark Island*, I remember very vividly—'full of grace and guts,' I said. There were many other names in 1952 which do not survive in later publishers' lists, though Giovanni Guareschi's *Don Camillo* has achieved celebrity.

R. C. Hutchinson was so obviously a novelist of immense gifts; that I have found his *Recollection of a Journey* 'a fine novel, perhaps a great one' reflects no particular credit on me. Nor do I pride myself on my discrimination in dismissing Frederick Rolfe's *The Desire and Pursuit of the Whole* as 'a piece of malignant spitting at a number of not very impressive people by a creature of shabby nature and unbalanced mind which has lost what bite or significance it ever had and is now of Boeotian dullness'.

Other old enthusiasms revived by the appearance of new novels were for Rosamond Lehmann, *The Echoing Grove*, Henry Williamson, *Tales of Moorland and Estuary*, and Margaret Kennedy, *Troy Chimneys*. Finally, in March 1953, just before leaving the *Sketch* (which folded up not long after), I gave a hearty welcome to Audrey Erskine Lindop and a respectful one to Hemingway's last novel, *The Old Man and the Sea*.

That was all I found in those six years and it seems now a dismal record, though probably not more so than the years immediately before them or the epoch of the proletarian novel, better called the lower middle-class novel, which was to follow them, with its rooms at the top and Saturday nights and Sunday mornings. Has anything, I wonder sourly in this year of 1973, *really* happened in English fiction since Conrad, Galsworthy, Lawrence (I suppose), Huxley, Forster (I suppose), the early Compton Mackenzie and perhaps a few of their minor but still considerable contemporaries like C. E. Montague, Maurice Hewlett, M. P. Shiel, Katherine Mansfield, Virginia Woolf, Arthur Machen, the earlier Maugham, H. G. Wells, Oliver Onions, Arnold Bennett or Kipling (for *Kim* and the short stories)? I would like to add wistfully the name of May Sinclair, one of the best woman novelists since the Brontës, though she is fashionably forgotten as a 'magazine writer'.

In any case what, in those six, or in the twenty succeeding years, has been published to compare with the work of any of those I have mentioned? I know all the defensive answers: I saw them through the clear glass of youth; it is my perceptions which have grown duller with age; we are all notoriously apt to look back in literature instead of forward. But I would still settle for just one novel to be set beside the weakest of Conrad's, the poorest of D. H. Lawrence's, *Kim* or *Sinister Street*. Just one and I would kill all my prejudices and greet the unseen with a cheer. But it does not exist now any more than during the period in which I was professionally engaged in searching for it.

CHAPTER THREE

Last of the Gypsies

[1]

I WOULD not have been human if I had looked only to the present and future and did not sometimes try to follow again the pursuits which had attracted me before the war. It was in doing so that I realized what a cleavage the war had made in mine as in most lives. Some interests which had been passionately followed by me in pre-war years, like the Circus and Gypsies, now became subjects for books, hobbies if you like, studies for research and only occasionally for personal contact.

The particular circus with which I had travelled so happily for several tenting seasons until the very day of the declaration of war, Rosaire's, was irrevocably broken up. The Count Rosaire and his eldest son Aubrey were dead, Ivor, who had been in the army, was working for Chipperfields, some of the girls had married and left the show, and although Dennis the wire-walker made a last attempt to turn out the big tent with the remainder of the family, he abandoned it after one season and, except for occasional visits in winter, I lost touch with him and his brothers and sisters and that splendid matriarch the Countess. Also I found when I met evidences of it in London that the *cult* of the circus was a most disagreeable business. It was one thing to laze through the English counties living in a trailer-caravan on the tobers of the Rosaires, hearing their story and observing their eventful life, it was quite another to be claimed as a fellow enthusiast by the members of an absurd institution called the Circus Fans Association, to visit by invitation Bertram Mills's circus at Olympia or Tom Arnold's in Islington, and hear the gossip not of the circus people themselves (as I was used to doing) but of the addicts of the ring, the collectors of old programmes and pictures, the members of a pseudo-artistic religion whom I found obsessed and boring.

It is true that with one of them, a fruity old character named Bill Meadmore, I collaborated in three books of circus interest, *The Sawdust Ring*, *The Circus Book* and *Buffalo Bill: The Legend, the Man of Action, the Showman*; it is true that when motoring out of London I never saw a circus poster without finding the show; but I had sadly to admit that the pre-war magic was gone, that having once put it into a book I had lost it for the rest of my life.

This was not quite true of the gypsies. I had lived and travelled with them in a more intimate and close-knit sense than I had with the circus, studied their history and their language, known love and fellowship with them and felt understanding with their very illiteracy, and sympathy with them as—I used the all too hideously fashionable phrase—a persecuted minority. I had made myself one of the *rais* who from Borrow onwards, with a greater or lesser degree of charlatanism, have gone among them and claimed to learn their secrets, I had written a novel about them, *Glorious*, which was published in the year of war and remained more or less unread. and I now wanted to put all I knew and felt about them, not into fiction, as I had done, but into a truthful reminiscent book of revelation. I drove down to Kent to find them round Tenterden as I had met them in 1939, and westward to Worcestershire, where I had known them in 1940; I broadcast about them on several occasions and I succeeded after a long pursuit in finding my dear illiterate friend Ted Scamp, who had travelled with me in the first snowbound months of war in a horse-drawn wagon. In 1948 I published the results of all this in *The Moon in My Pocket* and followed it with a book of short stories and prose sketches called *A Few Gypsies*. I was a member, though not an enthusiastic one, of the Gypsy Lore Society, a somewhat didactic institution centred in Liverpool, and I wrote a preface to *A Book of Gypsy Folk-Tales* by its secretary Dora E. Yates.

If today I have lost my deepfelt interest in Romanies, it comes from causes extraneous to myself and my passionate wish to defend them from their numerous enemies with the only weapons I can use—words. The race has degenerated so fast during the last twenty years, many times faster than their gradual decay since the time of Borrow, Samson and Groome, the greatest of the *rais*, that now there is scarcely a man or woman left in the British Isles who can claim to be as much as one-third Romani, and even the word *didakai* or half-caste is flattering to the mob of motorized caravanners or scrap metal merchants claiming to be members of a once proud, secret and enchanting race sprung from the East. For the first time that pretentious claim by sentimental ladies in Kensington 'my grandmother was a gypsy' might just as well be true for all its silly romanticism.

During the years I am recalling I had a few contacts with the gypsies, as I shall recall, and even today I never go into Kent without discovering Ted Scamp and his wife, now house-dwelling grandparents, and remembering with them (as grey-beards will), the times when all the trees were green. But to say that in London I returned to my pre-war absorption in Romani life would not be true.

[2]

I am writing here grandly about motoring, as though in 1946 I was what is meant today by a car-owner. In fact I possessed an Opel whose price *new* had been £110 when hundreds of them were forced by the Germans on to the British market before the war to earn foreign currency. In 1938 and 1939 I had driven it in England and Europe and, when petrol was no longer obtainable in 1940, had run it into an open-ended barn in Kent where it had lain until my release in 1946. It now looked nearly as good as new and ran smoothly and quite fast. I did a great deal more touring in Great Britain, Scandinavia, France and Switzerland, and finally replaced it in 1952 after fifteen years of trusty service.

The use I made of it in London in those years seems to me today scarcely credible though I am speaking of no more than two decades ago. To leave it in an open garage not two hundred yards away cost fifteen shillings a week, but often I did not bother to put it under cover but let it remain outside my house all night or all day without interference or reproach. I drove it to any part of London, leaving it at the door wherever I went —even to offices in Fleet Street or the City in the daytime. Parking metres had not, of course, been invented because there was plenty of room and breathalysers, of which in my sober maturity I approve, would have seemed to us in those days a Wellsian and macabre interference with the liberty of the individual. I can remember driving the Opel from Doughty Street to the Fitzroy or the Wheatsheaf, drinking all the evening and overloading it with friends to take back to my flat, all without any sense of guilt or fear of penalty. And do not let anyone lecture me on the immorality of this today. Motoring consciences had not yet been developed.

So the Opel was a direct link with my life before the war as other objects and interests failed to be. I no longer wanted to spend whole evenings on a darts board in a country pub as I had done so often once—there were too many people of interest to meet, too many long and seemingly worthwhile conversations to hold, too much entertainment to accept, plays and films to go to, comic episodes to witness and stories to hear. And anyhow there were too many middle-class intruders (as I chose to consider them) on the proletarian community of the darts board.

I no longer wanted to search bookshops for bargains—I could now afford to add to my collection the books I wanted without gathering others simply because my experience as an antiquarian bookseller told me they were cheap. I relied on chance and observation to add to the English watercolours and antique oddments I collected and I had no time to race about the countryside seeking them, though news of a country auction drew me as infallibly as ever. In other words I relied now on the excitements of my own profession, and the post and telephone which fed them, for the amusements of every day. To sell a short story for a large fee, then to broadcast the same story disguised, to 'do features' for weekly papers as when I spent a weekend in a holiday camp at Billy Butlin's invitation, or motored down to Marseilles to write a story about that supposedly wicked city. These were no more part of a writer's business than bookselling had been, but at this time they seemed more relevant and certainly more entertaining.

The holiday camp particularly was an experience. It was on the Yorkshire coast, the most impressive and populous of them all, and Billy Butlin himself was there that week-end. It is easy to jibe about holiday camps and other such useful institutions and I refrained from doing so, only noting one small grotesque incident which I found irresistible.

'How,' I asked Billy Butlin as we stood in a huge crowded parish hall of a bar named as all the identical bars were named after its scheme of mural decoration—The Parisian, The Georgian, The Victorian or The Hula Hula Bar. 'How do you get them out when it's time to close? Or don't you have to?'

'You'll see,' promised Butlin and by God I did.

At ten twenty-five on the dot there entered a comic procession, a file of camp leaders and funny men behind a big drum played by an even funnier man in clown's drag. They marched round the room, each holding the waist of the man in front and singing, as I had heard the Sally Army sing on a London street—

> Come and join us!
> Come and join us!
> Come and join our happy throng!

Before they had completed their hilarious progress round the room every man jack in the place was holding on to the waist of the one in front, grandmas, mums, dads and daughters, and yelling the chorus as the drum led the way artfully towards the doors. In a few minutes the bar was empty.

'See how it's done?' said Butlin or one of his circle. I did and appreciated it. Better, at least, and less painful than all that bellowing of 'Time!' which is such a part of the British way of of life.

The journey to Marseilles to write a feature on the city for *Illustrated* was no less memorable, because I asked Beverley Nichols to accompany me in the Opel and we went through Paris, where the shops were stacked with food and we could scarcely believe that *patisserie* with cream and chocolate and luscious *pâté feuilletée* could be openly displayed after our own stealthy and rare sales of manufactured sweetmeats. Beverley took me to see Edward Molyneux, whose name was still the greatest in the jealous world of dress-designing, and I found him a gentle and modest man, proud only of his fine collection of paintings. I met, too, at a typically Anglo-Parisian party, Nancy Mitford who had then published only one novel, *Pursuit of Love*. I had not read it or at that time written unforgivable if sincere reviews of Nancy Mitford's work, so the meeting passed without incident.

I was giving up cigarette smoking and so was unbearable as a travelling companion, and Beverley left me appropriately at Avallon while I drove on to Marseilles. It was during that visit that I saw the sand-dunes which were then all that was left of the Vieux Port and decided that I would write a novel about the Germans' destruction of that ancient and colourful slum. (I did so in 1953, *Seven Thunders*, and it was the first of my books to be filmed.)

That was the first journey I made after the war, and since I had soldiered in Africa and the East and not in Europe, it was a continuation of my pre-war travels having no relationship with the more recent Movement Orders and troopships. I saw little difference in France or the French people, little evidence of the hardships or (except in the Vieux Port) of the destruction they had suffered. I returned to London talking rather cynically about it.

But such excursions were rare. I could not recreate the irresponsibility of the pre-war years for then, whenever I received a cheque for more than about thirty pounds, I would without hesitation drive down to Dover to cross the Channel and make for some European city, leaving behind my flat, my unsatisfied creditors and my unfulfilled undertakings. My fortnightly review in the *Sketch* was now a hindrance to travel, so was my household, a more ambitious one, and the necessity to do a daily stint of writing. In spite of such sobering influences I enjoyed my first year back in London, determined as I was to rise above shortages and irritations and to regard as comedy the efforts of the Government to be a frugal and severe stepmother to us all.

[3]

In one other respect I continued to cultivate the ambitions of pre-war, that of broadcasting. I suppose those years after 1946 were the last in which 'steam radio', as it became irreverently called, kept its supreme popularity among all forms of entertainment. Television was beginning to outpace it but had not yet succeeded in making it appear a fuddy-duddy form of amusement. I know that it still has its adherents, who feel a loyalty to the medium which television fails to inspire, but then broadcasting was at its height—or should one say breadth?— and the names of its heroes were household words as no pop singer or Frost or Muggeridge now succeeds in being. A talk —ambiguous term—could make a man famous overnight, a short play could establish him as a dramatist and musical reputations were made all too easily. Living in London, I decided, could only be justified by taking advantage of this and I set myself to do so.

I had first broadcast from Savoy Hill in 1925 and recalled the incident in *The Numbers Came*:

> Broadcasting then was not without its vicissitudes. The first time I talked was on Buenos Aires and announced by Stuart Hibberd I stood at a microphone at one end of a large studio, while the members of an orchestra who had been playing before I began, and would bash on regardless afterwards, remained seated. There was much play with red lights and when I had finished one of the players left his place and, coming down the room, said he knew Buenos Aires and had I ever been to Fanny's Bar? As Fanny's, or the Phoenix Bar, was a notorious hang-out for whores I was horrified, thinking his question had gone through the headphones of thousands of listeners. No rehearsal was required from a speaker then or for several years afterwards and timing was a chancy matter. One talk I gave was four minutes short, which was too much for even Stuart Hibberd's composure and ingenuity. On another occasion when there had been an earthquake in the Azores I was asked during the morning whether I could talk about the islands after the six o'clock news that night. I agreed and hurried to the reading room of the British Museum to find out something about them. But it was one of the two days in the year when the reading room was closed for cleaning and the only book I could get hold of that day which mentioned the Azores was Lady Brassey's *Voyage of the Sunbeam*, which described a call made there in the 1870s. On this information I gave my talk and was congratulated on a piece of smart topicality.

But since then I had written radio plays (one about a ghost in a train was cancelled because of a railway accident on the day for which it was scheduled), jockey'd a number of discs, and given talks galore. Now I met during a visit to Sussex a character called Jack Dillon, who was a radio producer, and suggested to him a programme on gypsies. He was enthusiastic about the idea—more so than I was who knew something of gypsy elusiveness—and I took him and a party of technicians down to Worcestershire for the peapicking. The programme was completed after several days of mild hysteria and broken promises which Dillon *could* not understand, and was broadcast in due course. Charity Fletcher, who had a little reputation for *dukkerin* (fortune-telling) read my hand before the microphone and for weeks afterwards was besieged by motorists who had heard the broadcast, discovered where she was and wanted to cross her palm with silver. 'Liza Lock sang and there was a good deal of talk about hedgehogs and the open road. But I felt this was a kind of treason to my friends, who thought nothing of the sort and were delighted at the perks, but none the less treason because it exposed their illiteracy without revealing their unique and valuable qualities.

I did some more programmes with Jack Dillon, writing one about the Sydney Street Siege which was not a bad reconstruction of events. But the atmosphere in Broadcasting House and in the little pubs around it where the staff drank garrulously for long and boring sessions eventually became tiresome and I was content to read short stories of my own for Roy Campbell, surprisingly in charge of that department, and broadcast on several occasions for *In Town Tonight*, a topical weekly programme said to provide those who spoke on it with immense publicity. (It may have done so for those already well known. It did nothing for me because I am naturally, if I may use the word, unpublicizable.)

All this, and the *Sketch* articles, and the attention attracted by my book *Wilkie* which Somerset Maugham made his choice of the year in the *Sunday Times*, and a number of appearances in gossip or news columns, and the fact that I actually found myself sought after by publishers, gave me at least the illusion of success at that time such as I had never felt before and have certainly not known since. It was not very exciting. I knew only too well the faults of *Wilkie* and that I had not yet found the means of self-expression for which I was most suited. I had an uncomfortable suspicion that the ugly change which in fact came over the smiling face of fortune a few years later was already preparing itself then, and I have never craved madly for any degree of material success greater than that necessary to let me live by what I like doing most—writing.

Because a small share came to me at this time of the fortune left half a century earlier by my great uncle George Croft, who had been managing director of Charringtons the brewers, they were years of slightly more prosperity than their predecessors —or, alas, successors—so that my life in Doughty Street with Joseph and a number of old friends was a comfortable one. It is odd to remember that this period, when English people were most infuriated by the shortages, which they could not believe were inevitable, was for me one of plenty, and the ingenuity needed to keep it so was exhilarating rather than tiresome. Moreover those years in which to a future student of social history there were so many last gasps—of bourgeois prosperity, of conventional Christianity, of private ownership, of Imperialism—were for me, and I believe a great many others of my background, the first years in which we had become aware, in any full sense, that politics were real, actual and potent and had some bearing on our lives. We had expected government to be evident and authoritative in war time—with peace we thought it should revert to being a matter for the newspapers to write leaders about, something to provide occasional scares and sensations to enliven our days. When Attlee's government did not recede into this comfortable background we were at first astonished, then irritated, till at last we began to realize that the Age of Political Man was upon us and we could no longer enjoy our private rebellions or our particular unconformities without belonging to something, moving in a certain direction, being *aware* of it all, even if we were not actually impelled to do something about it.

[4]

Though none of them were in evidence when I first came to London, I had a number of friends of no marked distinction, some of whom despised even my small pretensions to respectability, while others, by their way of life as Circus *omies* or Romanies, had no truck whatever with conventional standards. I was immensely proud of these, proof as they were that I had broken free of the limitations of my upbringing and gone out into the highways and hedges and known how to appreciate the fine spirits I found there. Since in this book I must inevitably introduce a number of persons whose names were—sometimes *are*—well known and lustrous, let me first rejoice in those that were neither.

Clifford Gibbs had got his rather grand name from Dr Barnardo's Homes, for he had been reared in one of these, the son of a Chinese father and English mother, neither of whom he had ever seen. I had known him before the war and was as proud as he was of the Military Medal he had earned as a Corporal in the Royal Armoured Corps in North Africa. He had been sent to Burma and taken prisoner by the Japanese, and suffered unspeakable tortures and humiliations because of his race, separated as he was from his fellow British. He had survived and, inwardly as inscrutable as a Conrad character, a little like Wang in *Victory*, he had married a blonde English girl and had an exquisite baby daughter whose godfather I became at a Sunday afternoon service in an East End Anglican church.

Clifford, who went about life methodically, was severely industrious and found the means of saving for his family even in those days of grudging wages. But he had a humorous cheerful side to his character and enlivened my flat during his weekly visits between office hours and his return to Durban Street, E.15. He was an expert wrestler and had earned the Judo black belt. Only from the depths of his character emerged sometimes the exotic or oriental; in speech and manner he was very much an Englishman, and it was strange to hear from his curved lips words that might have been used by any London ex-soldier. I am glad to have had his friendship throughout those years.

In contrast were two Irishmen—in contrast to one another as well as to Clifford Gibbs. I had known them first at separate periods of my life in the army and they never met. They were co-racial but it took an English observer to see them as this, for Tommy Ludlow the ex-Sergeant of Commandos with whom I had become friends in Madagascar was from the South, a strong Catholic and a staunch admirer of De Valera, while Stewart Hamilton, the ex-Marine Commando, was—by category at least—a Protestant from the North.

Of Stewart Hamilton I have already written in *The Licentious Soldiery*, though since doing so I have heard from his son that he is dead and have mourned that a man so immensely full of life and generous instincts and humour should have left us so young.

Tommy Ludlow came to see me at Doughty Street and drove with me into Kent from the home in Romford where he lived with his young wife, who in those days was trying to tame his wild nature into middle-class English ways. Looking back on my friendship with him, which started on a troopship bound from Madagascar to Durban and continued through the years I am recalling, I cannot remember anything we did but *talk*, and since I have come to live in Ireland I do not wonder at that. Our bunks hung side by side on the troopdeck and we began talking then, of life, religion, sex, our two such different countries, our separate experiences, our sharply differing views, our ambitions, indeed everything there was to talk about, and we continued the conversation in London, Essex and Kent. In spite of our garrulity or because of it I remember Tommy as a splendid companion, who taught me much about his people which has since served me well and saved me from the various forms of sentimentality which confuse Englishmen in their view of the Irish. Tommy, like most of his compatriots who joined the British Services during the war, was concerned with immediate conditions and prospects but never for a moment forgot his own country, for his patriotism was obsessional. He is one of the few lost friends of wartime about whom I still feel curiosity. Is he a respected English resident, the father of a close-knit English family, or has he reverted to being someone as uncontrollable as the Commando Sergeant who distinguished himself in our little war in Madagascar against the Vichy French? Or is he, like my other Irish friend, no more?

Yet another wartime friend, this time an ex-matelot called Bill, arouses no such curiosity for I have followed his career until now when he is married for the second time, a good citizen of Manchester. But then he promised no such serious future and in our first days in London, while we both perforce wore uniform, his sailor's rig making a puzzling contrast with my barathea, we did our utmost to maintain the best, or at least the rowdiest and most hell-raising traditions of the services, rolling from pub to pub, trying to make believe that peace had never come to curb us. Childish and silly behaviour of course, in one trying to settle down as a householder, novelist and critic, and behaviour calculated to raise antagonism and ridicule. I suppose I was crying over what I had lost and should never have again, the noisy reckless carefree companionship of the army. I have never, like other ex-soldiers, tried to return to it by attending regimental reunions and such. Once signed away at the Release Centre it was gone for good and such riotous evenings as those I spent with Bill could do nothing to compensate for it. But what the hell, I thought then, and think now; there was plenty of bright life left.

[5]

But there was one friend with whom reunion was difficult after the war and one I wanted most of all to see, the gypsy who had travelled half across Southern England with me in a horse-drawn caravan, Ted Scamp. I have told elsewhere of that journey and how it ended abruptly when he had gone as he had come, without fuss or explanation, back to his own people. For six years I had received no letter, which was not surprising since he could not read or write, but by devious report, through hearsay among the didakais I met in Kent, in which county he had usually travelled, I heard that he was married and had two children, but nothing more. So, as an escape from London and work and respectability, my search for Ted Scamp began.

I went first to Minster, near which Thanet village the wagons of Ted and his mother and brother had stood on a farm called Seven Score. Of the low-ceilinged pub in which I had first met Ted and from which we had started on our journey I learnt that the landlord had been dead several years. I saw the 'new people'—as innkeepers in the country are called for at least their first year of tenancy—but they had never heard of my gypsy family. A man who overheard my questions drew me aside to explain that the 'old lady', Ted's mother, was dead.

'You've never seen such a funeral as she had,' he said. 'There was every diddy in Kent, I dare say; they followed her in their hundreds.'

'What happened to the sons?'

'Left here soon afterwards and never been seen again.'

At Seven Score Farm the kindly cowman who had written letters for the family could tell me no more. There was none of the Scamp family in Minster, he said.

Knowing that Riley Scamp, Ted's patriarchal father, had twenty-four children, and that most of the women were mothers and some of them grandmothers, I realized that there was no shortage of relatives, but it was hard to know which to approach. One sister was married to a fruiterer in Sittingbourne and Ted had been on good terms with his gorgio brother-in-law, so I decided to approach him. I was met with a stone-wall incomprehension.

'Never heard of any of them,' said the fruiterer when I

mentioned the various names under which Ted, in the manner of most gypsies, hid his own. 'Don't know anything about any gypsies. Can't tell you what I don't know, can I?'

I began to understand something of that conspiracy of silence which is the protection of all nomads. My motives for inquiring were not even demanded and if I had explained them they would not have been believed. Long, anguished experience has taught this furtive race that any house-dweller asking questions is suspect. Even if he is not a policeman his motives are probably hostile and no good can come of trusting him.

Then one August afternoon on the main road to Maidstone I stopped my car at the sight of a wagon pulled on the wide grass verge and was soon in conversation with a family of travellers. They were some of the Smiths, fairly pure-blooded and cognisant of gypsy ways. It was almost impossible that Ted's movements, if not his actual whereabouts, should be unknown to them, but I knew it would be foolish to approach the subject too directly.

When we had exchanged the usual gossip of the tans and I had shown myself well acquainted with their people, speaking familiarly of those I had seen recently, giving and receiving news of births and deaths and using my quota of Romani words to demonstrate that I could *jin* the *pooka*, I was handed a piece of paper by the father of the family.

'This letter came for me,' he said. 'Tell us what it says, will you, bor?'

It was a typewritten letter from some board or council, advisory committee or trust, some official, semi-official or unofficial (who can distinguish?) body which was apparently trying to canalize, direct, organize or distribute casual or seasonal agricultural labour, the sort of thing which the modern householder takes seriously as an outcome of the welfare state. It told Mr Ebby Smith that for hop-picking this year he was to report to such-and-such a farm on such-and-such a date.

'Well,' said Mr Ebby Smith, smiling with pleasure. 'Isn't it nice of them people to write to me? Do you know, rai, this is the first letter that's come for me in five years? We people do like to get a letter, and I'm pleased they should have troubled to write. Of course I shall go to Horsmonden for hop-picking as I've always gone but still, it was nice of them to write.'

If only house-dwellers, I thought, regarded such missives as sanely. But house-dwellers have not the Romani instinct for freedom.

It was then that I made my inquiry. Could Ebby Smith tell me anything of my friend Ted Scamp?

It was as though I had explained by this question the thing that had been puzzling them since I had stopped my car—why I had come to talk to them. It was as though now at last they perceived my sinister motive. Their manner changed at once.

'Don't know him,' said Ebby. 'Never heard the name.'

'Can't say, I'm sure,' added his wife sharply.

Our pleasant conversation ended abruptly. By my simple demand I had outraged their sense of good manners. I was no longer to be trusted.

But the letter they had shown me gave me an idea and during the next few weeks I visited a number of offices in the market towns of East Kent in the hope of tracing one of Ted's names. In these offices, I gathered, there was a great deal of planning and organization; from them advice was dispatched, labour directed, farmers notified, inspectors of this or that sent out. I heard typewriters tapping blithely as lists were made up and rotas, card-index systems, files and letters received attention. Their precise object I never discovered; they were concerned I think, with the distribution or concentration of something or other—it may have been labour. And in each of them were impressive lists of what I learned to call 'migratory agricultural workers'. These I was permitted to consult after I had explained my purpose to various young ladies, but all in vain. Whatever Ted had become since he walked away from my wagon that day before the war he was not a listed 'migratory agricultural worker'.

Months passed in which I inquired from every travelling

family I met where Ted Scamp might be found, protesting that I was no gavver or gavver's nark, that I wished him well and only wanted to find him again because we had travelled together. Down in the Weald, across the levels which run from the foot of the North Downs to the Romney Marshes, I stopped at pubs in which I knew the gypsies met. From the Beaneys, a didakai tribe headed by old Bill Beaney who had a voice like a bull, from the Brazils scattered since the death of Redpaunch their chief, from the Bartons driving by on their totting carts, from the deep Romani Hildings and Emmetts—from all I asked the same question, to be met with ingenious evasion, deliberately false information or embarrassed silence. Some would admit that they knew Ted.

'Know him well. Course I do. Old Riley Scamp's son. Next to youngest, isn't he? Married a Lee from Thanet way. Yes I know him.'

'Where do you think he might be?'

'Ah, that I couldn't say.'

'Know where he goes for hop-picking?'

'Can't say I do.'

Others would never have heard the name, or 'didn't know anything about other travellers, but kept to themselves as you might say', or had heard that Ted had 'gone over Essex way' or 'down towards Wales'. Yet others would set their lips, shake their heads and say nothing at all.

News came at last by chance, and a very lucky chance at that. One night, motoring home late, I saw two young men by the roadside thumbing—a good American phrase—thumbing a lift. Even during their moment in the headlights of the car I saw that they were gypsies and pulled up. During the run which followed I startled them by speaking Romanes.

'Where did you learn to rokker?' they asked.

'I've been on the drum.' The drum is the road.

'What, you a traveller, then?'

'No. But I was with a Romanichal.'

'You were? Who was that?'

I told them.

'When did this happen?'

I explained.

'Where did you go?'

I traced our itinerary. It seemed that they were satisfied for one of them said, 'You must be the book writer, then.'

I admitted it. Even so I had little hope of information but it seemed that my credentials were now established.

'Seen Ted lately?' one of them asked.

'Not lately,' I said, thinking of the thirteen years which had passed.

'My wife's sister's married to his brother.'

'I see.'

'Ted'll come this way for the scroops (hops).'

'Will he? Which pub does he use?'

'The Woolpack. Just up the road here. Don't know whether you'd call it Goudhurst or Curtisden Green. He'll be there any week-end in hop-picking time.'

'Good. I'll see him.'

I am not sure now whether I wholly believed this information, but it was good enough to test. And on the first Sunday of the hop-picking season I drove out to the Woolpack Inn.

There is a broad triangle of grass in front of this old house and a curve of driveway up to its doors. On that bright September morning the driveway was crowded with the vehicles of the hop-pickers and little grass was visible, for a hundred or two people were crowded together enjoying the sunlight and the beer, squatting on the ground or standing in groups. There were the pallid cockneys whose skins had not yet begun to redden and peel, there were a few people from the village and there were the nomads, the gypsies, didakais, gorgio vandwellers and a few of the road's brotherhood, pram-pushers and tramps who come to the hop-gardens for a fortnight or so to earn money for their annual bacchanals. It was lively, noisy and delightful, a holiday, a beery *fête champêtre*.

Sitting in a remote corner I saw Ted Scamp. His face

seemed more lined, stronger, more angular, but his thick black hair, his beautifully regular teeth, his slim muscular body, his quick faun's smile, were all unchanged. In a moment we were remembering sentimentally our journey together, this misadventure, that moment of relief; and the years between, the war, the tiresome annoyances of peace, were forgotten.

So that night we gathered round the wood fire by Ted's tent. It was eleven o'clock or more but none of us wanted to part for the night. Lily, Ted's wife, 'one of the Lees' as my informant had rightly said, was making a vast pot of tea for us all.

'You haven't got a wagon now?' I asked Ted.

'Had one, last winter. Nice trailer, it was, and a decent lorry to pull it. I was yogging (wood dealing) round your way, too. But the trailer was burnt.'

One needs to know a little of Romani life to understand the whole significance of that. Not only a man's home with everything in it is destroyed but probably his capital as well.

'Much money in it?' I asked.

'All I had.'

There was no glumness in his manner. He was smiling, perhaps a little grimly and Lily was not, apparently, listening. The disaster was of the past and had no significance for them now.

He went on talking not of the fire which had destroyed his own wheeled home and all his possessions, but of fire the preserver and destroyer both, as the gypsy understands it.

From that evening and for the last twenty-five years I have, as they say, kept in touch while Ted has become a grandfather and a householder in Canterbury. I do not plan to 'let him slip away' again—indeed it will be I who is likely to do that first.

CHAPTER FOUR

Outsiders and 'In' People

[1]

ALTHOUGH in this series of books I use my own life as a clothes line on which to hang the smalls of people and experiences, at this point I must treat it as something more, since only by allowing full play to the first person singular can I light up the portraits of others I knew at that time, others who for one reason or another are well worth recalling. For the first six years after the war, for the only time in my life, I was caught up in surroundings and among people considered by the victims of journalistic pressure to be socially, or artistically, or sometimes politically eminent, people whose names made headlines in popular newspapers or yet more noteworthily, appeared in discreet paragraphs of Court and Society news. These were not associations of my own choosing but once committed I found great charm and likeability even among stars of the stage or literature, even among peers and politicians, as I might have expected to find. Much of the charm was professional and rubbed off in a crisis, but much of it was natural.

Essentially I was, as usual, an observer. As in other forms of exploration, I made a few lasting friends, but in general I was never at home among those who erected social barricades or those who enjoyed living behind the hoardings on which their names were displayed. I entered the fairground with gusto; I enjoyed playing there. I pushed forward on occasion and was not above taking pleasure in my own small share of limelight. But I did not pretend to be more than an intruder whose manners and enunciation were not eccentric enough to be noticeable, whose origins needed no concealment or any of that inverted snobbery, fashionable in those years, of miner's cottage or city slum beginnings.

This produced a kind of mild schizophrenia in me, but I would have sworn at the time (and it might have been true) that my natural habitat was the public bar, my true associates the semi-illiterate, humorous friends of the past and of the army, and certainly these raised in me a fierce pride in having achieved their confidence, and I delighted in their deliberate unconformity. (Perhaps this was a kind of vanity—*I* had found them and it was *my* perception which appreciated them. I hope not. I was conscious of nothing of the sort.) Yes, these were my friends and the others, the well known and the cultured, were exhibits in an expensive well-stocked zoological garden. But it could not be as simple as that. Many of the gypsies and ex-servicemen, the pub acquaintances and semi-criminals were bores in spite of their promising categories, and many of the celebrities were enchanting people. However, I had invited the dilemma in my own life and cheerfully decided to live with it and to meet people of both extremes on their own ground. This, for six happy years, I did.

I must make it clear that these new acquaintanceships, whether literary or social, did not come about through any family connections or from any distinction earned as a writer. In fact it was through the interest of certain friends of long standing who considered me, in spite of my dubious backstairs associations, a suitable subject for social—advancement, was it, or reform?

Compton Mackenzie, still an unknighted novelist with strong if not dangerously rebellious habits of thought and expression, had shown himself the kind of friend—rare in the jealous world of authorship—who not only as a critic commended my work but did practical things to help my career. I had spent my embarkation leave at his home on the island of Barra and he now, with manifest foolhardiness, invited me to the Savile Club and was actually prepared to put me up for membership. Moreover he told me that when he had first been approached to write the story of the Indian Army in the war and it had seemed to involve too much travel and time for him to undertake, he had suggested me for the job.*

I could have told him—bless his kindness—that I was as unqualified for one as for the other, though perhaps I would have let him down more certainly as a member of the Savile than as a war historian since my interest in India would have been fully engaged.

Monty Mackenzie, too, had his share of this kind of schizophrenia. He never completely lost his affection, if not respect, for the Establishment in the shape of his old school, St Paul's, and his Oxford college, Magdalen, while he kept always his courtly manner, his pride in his part in the First World War, his love for the English countryside, his concern with his own good citizenship and royalist enthusiasm which culminated in his acceptance of a title. These scarcely blended with his championship of Edward VIII at the time of his abdication, his loathing for Stanley Baldwin, his Scottish Nationalism, his defending of certain offenders against the law, his gift of ridicule which mocked all pomposity (even Winston Churchill's), his rebelliousness and his occasional humorous contentiousness.

If I am right in diagnosing double-sidedness in Monty Mackenzie's character, a diagnosis he would surely refute or ridicule, it was the pro-Establishment face of it that was uppermost when he returned from the East to settle at Denchworth Manor in Berkshire. I went down to stay with him and found him in squirarchal splendour in a house which might have been created as the famous last home of a celebrated British writer, Kipling's Bateman's, Hardy's Max Gate, Meredith's Flint Cottage. His contemporaries, Brett Young and Hugh Walpole, had set up establishments of similar purpose at Graycombe House in Worcesertshire and Brackenburn in

*Sir Compton Mackenzie, it is well known, agreed to do the book and produced *Eastern Epic*. He wrote: 'Since October 1st 1946 I have travelled over 8,000 miles by sea, made over sixty flights totalling about 30,000 miles, driven over 9,000 miles by road and travelled over 3,000 miles by train, over 50,000 miles in all and 101 different beds.'

Cumberland respectively, but nowadays the custom is dying out, probably because few living writers rate more than a council house apiece and one cannot well imagine pilgrimages being made to the home of a Grand Old Man at number 27 Attlee Villas, Coulsdon. But here was Monty Mackenzie in a manor house which went back, as he said, to mediaeval times and had been *modernized* in the seventeenth century. It had its share of folklore and Amy Robsart had spent her last night here. Monty's library was housed in a tithe-barn and there was every appearance of permanence since he had moved all his possessions here from Barra. But I felt as I saw it all that in spite of the undoubted charm of the house, its history and its setting, it was not *right* for the volatile genius, the island-lover and romantic who was living there. For this feeling I cannot account except by the most blatant use of hindsight, but it was strong and I was in no way surprised when, after the failure of his Appeal against a decision of the Revenue authorities which made him liable for a very large sum in Income Tax through (I still feel) a most unjust decision, he decided to sell Denchworth Manor and live in Edinburgh, spending his summers in south-western France.

On that visit to Denchworth Manor I met for the first time (since by a series of coincidences she had been absent whenever I had visited Monty) his first wife Faith. I knew her books and found her a princessly woman—though by this I do not mean that anything in her manner was regal or over-dignified. She compelled interest not by being assertive but by the sheer liveliness and point of her wide-ranging conversation. She had a drawing-room of her own at Denchworth and showed me among its old delicate furniture and faded brocades the ghost of a small bird—a white canary. White canaries, for all I know, may be common creatures but the one I heard and saw on Faith Compton Mackenzie's finger, was the first known to me and haunts my memory.

My friendship with Monty was happily to continue and there would come a time when, at considerable sacrifice, he would prove its immense value to me. Mine would have been a poorer and a duller life without him.

But as he has grown older that pro-Establishment side of him has overwhelmed entirely the old caustic Monty of years ago, until in the later volumes of *My Life and Times* one finds praise and personal appreciation showered on everyone he meets and one seeks in vain for the critical tincture. This is all very well and renders him not only a Grand but a supremely amiable Old Man. Where, I cannot help asking, is the author of *Vestal Fire* and *Extraordinary Women*? The raconteur who made me ill with laughter at his impersonations of Hall Caine, D. H. Lawrence and Francis Brett Young? Silenced by the benevolent tattle of old age.

[2]

William Somerset Maugham, whom I met at that time, was so different a man that it was absurd, as some attempted to do, to bracket the two of them and add E. M. Forster as the Three Wise Men of English Letters.

My acquaintance with Maugham—it was scarcely more— was heralded by so much noise and name-dropping among lesser men and women who knew him that when I met him he seemed surprisingly unformidable. 'Willie Maugham told me ...', 'Willie has invited me ...', it never stopped, and a picture emerged of an immense Mandarin, as in Graham Sutherland's portrait, a cruelly witty ogre who could produce tears of chagrin in his guests, living in grotesque luxury in a large villa in the South of France, soured and embittered by the burdens of a long unsatisfied life, who never spoke without helplessly stuttering (an important part of all the impersonations in the 'Willie' anecdotes), grossly intolerant and malicious, especially towards the young, of whom he was supposed to be jealous.

Nothing, in my judgement, could have been farther from the

OUTSIDERS AND 'IN' PEOPLE

truth. I met him, at his invitation, several times in London and later in the South of Spain and I found an amiable and kindly man, encouraging not only me but other younger writers, a man in evident good health and high spirits notable in one of his age (he was then in his seventies). The sour ogre slapping people down for an incautious remark, the grand-scale snob and cruel ringmaster who dominated people about him, the secretive homosexual still suffering from the loss of his only lover, the American Gerald Haxton, none of these characters who appeared in the silly little stories that pursued him seemed to me to have much relationship with the truth.

He was homosexual, of course, and even used the vocabulary of London queers. He had a sharp and ruthless sense of humour which produced dry and sometimes rather scathing remarks, but he did not try to wound as he so easily could have done. His stutter was admirably controlled and for long periods unnoticeable. He was far more a *writer* than appeared in the popular anecdotes, far more devoted to literature than his visitors at the Villa Maroc seem to have perceived, since they saw him as a social lion rather than as the medical student of long ago who had decided to give his life to writing. But to me the quality he showed most plainly was that of kindness. He was not particularly tolerant, he was not easily approached or a public do-gooder of any kind, but his instincts, his actions, his words were essentially those of a kind and generous man, who built up defences to conceal this, as other men anonymously give to charities.

As a small example of this, which will seem trivial to those who do not know the tiresomeness to authors of being asked to inscribe their books, I quote the fact that Maugham not only spontaneously offered to write in all my copies of his novels but sat down before a stack of them in his suite at the Dorchester and not only signed them but added something to each. They are now, of course, very treasured possessions. Incidentally Norman Douglas found the perfect answer to insistent inscription seekers. Louis Golding asked him to adorn the flyleaf of

South Wind and he did so. '*Put something in it,*' says Louis. '*In what?*' *says Norman*. Maugham's inscriptions in that sharp firm handwriting of his were less curt.

His large face, lined and scarred by time, did not show emotion easily and I never heard him laugh outright. He did not even smile unless something positively amused him, least of all at a witticism of his own. He was cheerfully sardonic rather than easily amused, and a friendly listener rather than the tyrannical talker he was popularly supposed to be.

Towards the very end, I believe—for he was in his nineties when he most unwillingly died—he exhibited some of the embarrassing weaknesses of extreme old age and Alan Searle, his adopted son, had some painful years with him. I knew him only between 1946 and 1954 and in those years there was no sign of senility. As a writer he was a great story-teller and proved in *Of Human Bondage* that he could, as they say, write a novel with the best of them. His work, whether by intention or natural talent, was supremely entertaining and commercial and rightly he amassed a large fortune from it. His family affairs and disagreements will not, I think, be of much concern to the literary historian of the future, because talents such as Maugham's have a way of being cut down to size by posterity and he is unlikely to rank as one so important that every scrap of hearsay or recorded talk must be remembered. Neither as a novelist nor as a playwright did he exercise much influence on his time, but for me he was one of the heroic figures of literature who, since I was a boy, I have in some way revered, figures who did not shrink when I came to meet them—Kipling, Galsworthy, Chesterton, Belloc, Compton Mackenzie, Somerset Maugham.

[3]

I met Somerset Maugham through a remarkable woman named Lady Juliet Duff, remarkable in many respects, not least of which was the youthfulness of her appearance in what must have been, I recognize now, old age. This was so marked that when I met her daughter, Veronica Tennant, in Tangier later I tactlessly told her that I knew her sister Juliet, a gaffe that was clearly covered by David Herbert.

If Lady Juliet had been a Frenchwoman she would have been one of the great *salonnières*, though nothing could be more grotesquely improbable than Lady Juliet on a *recamier* couch giving literary At Homes. She was, however, that rare being, a woman who, herself uncreative, passionately loved literature, a woman whose interest was perennially aroused by new or promising writers. She must have been going through a parched time in the year when my novel *Wilkie* appeared for although she did not know me or anything about me, she wrote me a long letter of congratulation and sent a copy of the book to Somerset Maugham. Compton Mackenzie wrote of her:* 'Tonight I'm dining with Lady Juliet Duff which means an enchanting evening back in a civilized world ... Lady Juliet, who was a sister of Lord Lonsdale, kept that enchantment of once upon a time to the end. I count my friendship with her one of the cherished privileges of my life. To dine with her was to recapture youth.' If Monty Mackenzie could feel that, how much more did I, twenty years his junior? But Juliet Duff was what is called a spell-binder and there must be a place in literary history for women like her, who encouraged the writers of our generation and made us remember her when so many more prominent and mediocre women, like Barbara Castle and Eleanor Roosevelt, will have long disappeared from our memories. For her antecedents we must go back to the eighteenth century, to Martha Blount and Hester Thrale and others, since the only Victorian women who are known to have platonically befriended writers were writers themselves.

Another more dedicated, one might say more professional hostess who survived at this time, though she had ceased to give her famous luncheon parties at which young writers

*Compton Mackenzie, *My Life and Times*, Octave 8.

would be introduced to Somerset Maugham and Hugh Walpole, was Sybil Colefax, who in an almost literal sense hung on to life though crippled and twisted by arthritis ('like a bat', said Beverley Nichols who introduced me). It was cruelly apt, I thought, as I saw the contorted little figure with its elbow raised on high, and the voice which had once exchanged repartee with 'Willie' Maugham reduced to a senile croak, and all the light gone from the face that had launched a thousand best-sellers. I would have done well not to have met Sybil Colefax but kept the legendary vision of the great hostess at whose table every writer of the twenties and thirties had displayed his conversational wares.

A gleam of sunlit radiance was discernible in another woman whom I met at that time, but radiance in a different sense for it had more directly inspired writers. This was Bridget Patmore.

It was not through Somerset Maugham—I find the use of the familiar 'Willie' recalls those stage anecdotes in which everyone, however little known to the narrator, has a nickname and one is deafened by references to 'Larry' Olivier. 'Liz' Taylor, and 'Flo' Robson—it was not through Somerset Maugham that I met his nephew Robin, now Lord Maugham, He was then a young-looking literary tearabout, writing short stories published as fore-shortened novels and enjoying the *business* of writing in a way that very few of us are able to do. Everything he wrote had to be a film script and he spent endless time and money on the trappings of an important writer —secretaries, agents, lunches to editors, publishers or film directors—a very busy man. He talked well of people and events when they were outside his immediate pursuit of success and some of his stories about his Uncle Willie and his father, the first Lord Maugham, were devastatingly funny.

My friendship with Robin Maugham survives to this day, and survives in spite of something which would wreck almost any literary friendship, the fact that I do not admire Robin's writings and I do not suppose he has any more respect for mine. But he has a way of cropping up in unexpected places,

Cadiz, Tangier, Madrid, London, always vigorous and voluble, always exuberantly pleased to see his friends, often surrounded by uninteresting young men but never himself uninteresting. He is enthusiastic about his work, his life and his own activities, and although he makes no secret of it and shamelessly talks financial literary shop I do not find this irritating in him. It is obviously all such fun to Robin and when I see him off to the Far East to write a story about Mao or a film script about Buddhist monks, neither of which may come to anything, I know I shall be glad when he comes back.

But I am remembering those years immediately after the war when Robin was just beginning to write and to show himself a clever raconteur. We were together for a week-end at G. B. (Peter) Stern's cottage at Blewbury and I remember walking 'towards a gold-dust sunset down the owl-light in the lane' and talking not about his Uncle Willie or about film-rights, but about a forgotten novelist named J. D. Beresford whom he had known and about the village of Blewbury in which Kenneth Grahame had lived so that the stream of *Wind in the Willows* ran through Peter Stern's garden.

Peter Stern, though she was still writing vigorously and had yet to publish her novel about Stevenson's supposed son, in my mind belonged to that lively period before, during and immediately after the First World War, the period when Maugham himself led the popular field and women novelists all knew and talked about each other, Rebecca West, May Sinclair, Rose Macaulay, G. B. Stern, Clemence Dane, Sheila Kaye-Smith, Dorothy Richardson *et genus omne hoc*, none of them very *important* novelists, perhaps, but all loving books and 'new developments' and rivalry and country cottages, and all of them producing books which make most of the women novelists of today look tatty and superficial.

I had come to literary consciousness amidst a clamour of their names and rented one of the Cornish bungalows near Padstow which 'Sapho' Dawson Scott used to let to them. As I myself began to write I came to know all of them except perhaps the best writer among them, May Sinclair, who had already been confined in a mental home in which she died, like her contemporary Gilbert Cannan, twenty years later. Several of them had welcomed me in print as a newcomer and four of them had became my—more or less intimate—friends.

Peter Stern had been a successful writer and until about this time had lived in Albany and kept the necessary country cottage at Blewbury, in which village Margaret Steen also lived. Peter was Jewish as her novels brilliantly reveal but had recently become a Catholic. She loved good food and had a keen knowledge of wine; she talked well and cultivated a circle of friends of some notability as actors and writers. In later years she became afflicted with chronic obesity, but at the time when Robin Maugham and I stayed with her for that summer week-end in which the very countryside seemed to be that of *Georgian Poetry*, she was active and prosperous and still a well-known figure in stage and literary circles.

On a later week-end, when she had one of her secretaries at Mill Brook Cottage, we decided to spend the evening in dictating a one-act play together, instead of playing cards, doing the Mephisto crossword or talking. So dictate it we did, in two hours of enthusiastic effort, and saw it published in one of those series of plays for amateurs as *Gala Night at the Willows*. It has rarely been performed, demanding as it does an almost totally inebriated cast to make it convincing.

[4]

Since I am remembering writers of the time, though postponing descriptions of my contemporaries and juniors to a later chapter, I would like to recall several others who had in common their professionalism and devotion to their craft, which suggested that they had been more at home in the period pre-war when books were everything to us and did not have to compete with other forms of public entertainment like television. Professionalism was indeed all I demanded in a writer; I could stomach poor work and commercialism but not amateurishness.

So I remember meeting in a restaurant—after a party given by Rebecca West—a man whose name resounded just after the First World War, Gilbert Frankau (the author, one must inevitably add, of *Peter Jackson Cigar Merchant*). At the age of eighteen, when I read this book, I thought it was the greatest war novel of them all and learned by heart some of its purple passages. Gilbert Frankau was a somewhat gaunt exhausted-looking man who still wore the toothbrush moustache of a young officer in 1914–18, and was still writing novels. He told me, in fact, of the one he had coming out which he said was to be highly unusual. In a sense it was—the story of how the Devil himself becomes born into the body of an Eton boy and later lives devilishly. Frankau, who was then in his middle sixties, made me feel rather sad, not that he was a self-pitying man—he seemed to enjoy life—but sad as one feels when forced to realize that the heroes of boyhood become the bores of middle-age. His daughter Pamela, whom I met at the same party, was a highly spirited person, immensely popular with the older women around her, like them a writer who enjoyed literary gossip as much as any of them, and told delightfully funny stories about her friend J. B. Priestley. She, like Peter Stern, had become a Catholic and seemed anxious to make it known. I did not know her well but I remember that some years afterwards she had a big success with a novel *Road Through the Woods* and shortly after that died.

There were others who belonged to the Establishment of literature rather than the rag-tag and bobtail of my own age, and some of them were very established indeed, by inclination and temperament. H. E. Bates, for instance, though strictly speaking my contemporary, was so much a paterfamilias, a respected rather than an inspired writer, an industrious turner-out of good prose, that no one could think of him as anything but established.

He lived in what had been an artisan's cottage on the green at Little Chart near Ashford, but with the prosperity that had come after years of pre-war slogging he had ornamented it with a Georgian porch, added a luxurious bathroom and cultivated the garden to rival that of Beverley Nichols. I had known him since 1925 and have to confess that I always found him frigid and rather solemn, a man who brought out an occasional joke as though its gestation had been a labour of Sisyphus. ('The Lady's not for frying,' he said of Sheila Kaye-Smith when I told him her husband was a baronet and she would one day be Lady Fry.)

Before the war he had been quite a pleasant young man who had brought some of his progeny over to see my caravan and talked fondly of my native Kent which he had come to love—he was a Northamptonshire man by origin. But success during the war with his Flying Officer X books seemed to have given him a self-importance which I found difficult to take, and although, loyal to my own generation, I had given him what publicity I could in the *Sketch*, I found something which I considered pretentious in his home, his conversation and in his wife's open attempt to popularize the initials 'H. E.' as a sobriquet to match Wells's H. G. and Shaw's G. B. S. Or perhaps I was simply jealous of his sales. At any rate the attempts on both sides to be friends, or even welcoming acquaintances, were a failure, long before the events in my life of 1953 showed them to have been so.

'No,' he said as I have elsewhere recounted. 'Not water-colours. Everyone *starts* by collecting them.' And he glanced upward at one of the expensive prints of French masterpieces on his walls. About the garden when I had moved into the country, the house, the furniture (though not, I must admit, about the art of writing), he was equally admonitory. It was probably kindly meant but it did not endear him to me, nor did a neighbour who was a passionate devotee of his work who did not seem to embarrass him by years of adulation.

[5]

I dare say I was too concerned with the novelists, good or mediocre, whose names I had known since adolescence, that time when most of what one reads is remembered in after years and one has enthusiasms but no real discrimination. Two writers of public school novels, of which there were plenty before the 1920s, became known to me at this time, thirty years after the books by which they had first become famous had been published, books which in my 'teens had seemed immensely significant and exciting, Alec Waugh, as I have recounted, and Ernest Raymond, who gave a party at his home in Hampstead to which I was taken by one of his guests.

I had read nothing since *Tell England*, which for some reason had made me cry in 1922, though I knew that Raymond had continued to publish at regular intervals. I found him a cheery host and father, reminding me by something in his manner that he had been an army Chaplain. (He resigned his Orders in 1923.) Alec Waugh was at that party and I told him the story of how his father Arthur Waugh, the managing director of Chapman and Hall, had accepted my first novel because when he went home and read it to his wife (who as the wife of one writer and the mother of two was doubtless bored by books) she had said 'Go *on*, Arthur!' when he had paused. 'I'm having breakfast with my mother tomorrow,' Alec said when I told him this at Ernest Raymond's party, 'and I shall remind her.' How important it all seemed then, and the names of writers, and what was coming out next!

Alec himself gave a rather splendid party at the White House in which he had a flat and I met there for the only time one of the three poets who had reached such celebrity between the wars, not Auden whom I had succeeded in avoiding in spite of Monty Mackenzie's recommendation, nor Spender whom I had met once, but Cecil Day-Lewis who like Alec had been at Sherborne. In poetry as much a rebel as the other two members of what in the public mind was a trio, in life he had conformed with a better grace. I liked him and respected his work and professionalism.

Another giver of literary parties at the beautiful house near Sevenoaks where he lived with his then wife Chrystal, A. P. Herbert's daughter, was John Pudney. He and Chrystal both became friends of mine and remain so. At their home I met Harold Nicholson and his wife, Vita Sackville West, the former diffident and difficult except with friends of very long standing, chiefly much younger men, the latter, whose beauty had once been famous, sun-tanned and wrinkled by long seasons of gardening. Clearly I should have had to meet them years earlier to make more than polite small talk with them now, though Harold Nicholson was a frequent subject of conversation among my friends.

It is scarcely fair to count John Betjeman among these respected and established men and women, for at that time he was still, to use a tired but expressive term, an *enfant terrible* among writers, but a look through his entry in *Who's Who* today entirely obscures the early impishness and iconoclasm of his style. But for the title of an early book, *Ghastly Good Taste*, it is buried under the titles Royal Fine Art Commissioner, Governor of Pusey House, Hon. D. Litt., Hon. ARIBA, and of course CBE. I do not mean that John, whose friendship I still enjoy, has changed as a person; it is his public image which has grown unduly serious and reputable. He is as much given to gusty laughter as when I first met him in a public debate about spiritualism in the town of Newbury, to which we had both been invited by a charming man named Oldfield Box. John spoke thoughtfully and well and was popular among the members of the society. I became maddeningly Roman Catholic and adhered to the teaching of the Church on this subject, which as I understood it was that most supposed 'manifestations' were fakes and that if they were anything else they were, quite simply, the work of the Devil.

From this unpromising debate grew a splendid friendship

with Betjeman which has adorned my life ever since, right down to the recent occasion on which, at a party, he read the funniest bits out of an absurd book of pederastic verse he had discovered. The dirty old men of seventy years ago, it appeared, took their passions for little boys with fearful seriousness, except for one clergyman named Bradford who must surely have chuckled when he wrote *The Kiss*:

> He never had done it to Geoff, or to Guy,
> Nor to Arthur—not one of the three:
> And I thought that he never would, he was so shy!
> But he did it—he did it to me!

I do not forget the sheer delight in John's voice as he read out these ridiculous lines, or these by a schoolmaster named Nicholson:

> There is a Pond of pure delight
> The paidophil adores,
> Where boys undress in open sight
> And bathers banish drawers.
>
> There youth may flaunt its naked pride
> Unscathed by withering Powers,—
> Convention's narrow laws divide
> That swimming-bath from ours!

But even before I met him, John Betjeman had given a valuable boost to my novel *Wilkie* in the *Daily Herald*, for which he was then reviewing. He has always been a lovable man, generous with his time as with everything.

His wife—and is Penelope really known now as Lady Betjeman? I suppose she must be, but it sounds improbable—his wife is the daughter of Field-Marshal Chetwode and very much a character in her own right. When she is not riding about Spain on a donkey she is exercising her bright sense of humour on an enormous circle of friends among whom she is known as kind, talkative and original.

[6]

But there were more writers whom I met, or re-met at this time, and I do not wish to omit their names from this catalogue. C. P. Snow, of whom I have written exhaustively enough in *The Ghost of June*, was a plump commonplace man half university don, half civil servant, straining then towards literary success, deeply concerned with his press notices and not yet knighted. Nor had he yet married Pamela Hansford Johnson who at that time I thought was a good friend of mine, but he was already, as he told me emphatically, a member of the Athenaeum and the author of novels which I found all but unreadable, though I did not say so in my *Sketch* review.

A more interesting writer, and one who I think should rank with the first of contemporaries, was R. C. Hutchinson. I had read everything he had written and thought him as near an important novelist as this age can produce, but when I met him—at some party, I think; it might have been on my single attendance at a PEN Club gathering—I found myself quite unable to tell him so, which may have been just as well. He was refreshingly unlike a novelist in appearance or conversation, not in the least forbidding but not noticeably sociable either, a man only to be met through his books, as all good writers should be. On that same occasion—I'm sure it was at the new premises of the PEN Club which I never re-visited—I met another writer, whom I had not seen since he used to visit Charles Lahr's shop in a bowler hat, John Brophy. I have never taken newspaper reviews too seriously, believing with Joseph Conrad that they should be *measured* not read, but John Brophy's criticisms of early books of mine passed all bounds of common decency or fairness. As book after book appeared he reviewed them in different periodicals, *Liverpool Post*, *Time and Tide* and once in the *Daily Telegraph*, with remarks which were not criticism but compounded of personal malice and the pawkiest jealousy. Later when success came to him and films were made of his books all this disappeared and on the evening when he came to greet me at the PEN Club, of which I believe he was some sort of official, he did so with considerable heartiness.

'As a pabulum for tired minds, mental age ten,' I quoted from one of his less bitchy reviews, '*Blind Gunner* deserves to find a market. As literature it is shoddy and sham.'

He had not even the guts to stand by what he had written. 'You know, reviews get so sub-edited and cut, that they are often scarcely recognizable,' he said with an ingratiating smile. I left it at that.

Yet another rather curious figure whom I met in a bookshop which specialized in purchasing reviewer's copies was Edmund Blunden. I had known his poetry since *Georgian Poetry* days and several of his poems have been so often and so widely anthologized that I could scarcely help doing so. I wrote him a fan letter while I was in my early twenties and received an answer from Tokio University. There was scarcely a chance to learn or perceive anything of him in that crowded bookshop and I remember him only as a dim little figure in a soiled raincoat, with spectacles on his long sharp nose, who giggled helplessly whenever the bookseller spoke to him. Perhaps he had over-lunched or perhaps he found serious Mr Frank, the bookseller, irresistibly funny or perhaps it was a nervous giggle intended to show his bonhomie. I do not know. I have given up expecting poets to be quite complete as men.

Though another, a more considerable poet perhaps, was Richard Church who was certainly very much a man and, in his particular way, a great one. He has told how he came from a lower middle-class background (a greater encumbrance to a writer than a proletarian home which may be boasted of in any autobiographical note) and how, by years of industry and generous appreciation of others, he achieved independence, a family, an oast-house in Kent and, although he says nothing of this, the almost universal affection and regard of the literary world. One of the noblest men to rise from this metier, he was a good talker but not a showy raconteur, though his stories about W. H. Davies were both human and hilarious.

I am drawing to the end of this list of recognized and mostly older writers but not before I remember Rose Macaulay, a woman of most endearing eccentricity who was kind enough to come to my flat to sign the almost complete collection of her books. She was a notable figure at that time, greatly respected as a novelist but not escaping a hint of ridicule for her way of life. She had a small motorcar in which she hurried about London with such recklessness—or was it blindness?—that her passengers crossed themselves and gave thanks to God on alighting and, no less recklessly, she gave parties at which the most unlikely people were expected to know each other and one saw T. S. Eliot gripped by some desperate lady novelist, and other anomalies.

I went to one of these myself and have recalled it in *The Ghost of June*, but the occasion for me was more than merely farcical, since I met and enjoyed meeting Eddie March who died a few years later. He was perhaps the greatest friend to poets in the past hundred years, a dear little man whose sexless goodwill was evident in his face and conversation.

[7]

Two writers from my past, who have figured in previous books of mine, reappeared just then—Rhys Davies from his native Wales, and Louis Golding from the United States where he had spent most of the war. (But not all of it. Louis had planned a heroic return to London when he thought the bombing was over and arrived for the V bombs. In truly Louisian fashion he made the best of this and amused my circus friends one afternoon by saying he must return to London because this later form of bombing had provided him with 'the greatest emotional experience of his life'.)

Rhys did not change with the years but was still the solitary, quiet, industrious man I had known since 1925. He had achieved—or should one say he had been given—considerable recognition as a brilliant writer of short stories. He came to my flat several times but I was no nearer to understanding that recondite personality than I had been when we lived in neighbouring rooms in High Holborn, twenty years earlier.

Another writer who had achieved distinctions since I had last seen him in 1930, the year in which *Vile Bodies* and my first novel had come from his father's firm, was Evelyn Waugh. It certainly had not left him unchanged and, although he was nothing but courteous and friendly to me (I gave him for his novel *Helena* the *Sketch* prize for the best book of the year, which meant our appearance together on television), he had become something of a joke among most of his fellow writers. Penelope Betjeman told the astonishing story that when as godmother to one of his children she had suggested that she would not choose the conventional silver as a baptismal present because nowadays silver was difficult to keep clean, he had said rather tartly and quite seriously, 'I hope no child of mine will ever lack a servant to clean the silver.'

Evelyn Waugh, in fact, grew odd in his manner long before his last illness, but even if a trifle self-important he was never ungenerous. When I asked him if I could reprint a passage from *Decline and Fall* in an anthology, he told me to take the fee in cash to the nearest Catholic church and drop it in the poor-box. But like most literary humorists he did not show much inclination to humour in his private life. No one will believe me if I say that in his last years the creator of Lady Metroland and Agatha Runcible and Miles Malpractice became rather—dare one say it?—a bore; but it was so.

That closes my list of older or established writers whose acquaintance I enjoyed at that time but for one exception, the most important and the best of them all, who in my mind came very near to ranking with the great novelists of my young manhood when Conrad and Hardy were alive. This was Oliver

Onions of whom Compton Mackenzie wrote: 'I have never been able to understand why English critics failed to grasp his importance to the English novel and short story in the earlier part of the twentieth century.' Nor have I. But then I had the privilege—a rare one for he led a hermit's life in Wales—of meeting him and corresponding with him.

I say a hermit's life, but he was not alone, having married yet another author who was with him to the last, a prolific writer of women's novels named Berta Ruck. When in my first year on the *Sketch* I gave Oliver Onions the annual award (in the year before Evelyn Waugh) he apologized for not being able to make the journey to London and, delightfully, his wife came in his place.

Berta Ruck is Welsh—half by blood, wholly by nature—and has the gift of making everything Welsh, landscape, music, words, character, seem glorious. Utterly unlike the 'lady novelists' of her time (as apart from the 'women writers'), she has a sparkling sense of humour that must have made such tiresome bitches as Ruby M. Ayres sick with jealousy, if they ever met her. I would like to read at least a long essay on all those mistresses of women's fiction with sometimes hyphenated names like Elizabeth York-Miller or Mabel Barnes-Grundy, or the titled ones like the Baroness Orczy, the Baroness Von Hutton, and the Countess Barzcynska, or the romantic-sounding ones like Marie Corelli, or the midway-initial ones like Ethel M. Dell and Ruby M. Ayres. I am sure their lives would make excruciating reading. But dear Berta Ruck had nothing in common with them. She was totally unpretentious, proud only of Oliver Onions not of her large-selling books, witty and experienced but unspoilt by a cultivated sophistication.

At that *Sketch* luncheon when she was deputizing for her husband we got on—as they rather enigmatically say—like a house on fire and have continued to do so till now, and my reading of an autobiographical book, written incredibly I believe in her eighties but as witty and enthusiastic and proud of her country as her conversation—*A Trickle of Welsh Blood*.

A year or two later I met Oliver Onions himself, a salty, deep-running man, a writer of the most harrowing and beautiful ghost stories of our time, *The Beckoning Fair One* and *Phantas*, of the only historical novels which have utterly escaped from the descriptive woolliness of Scott and taken the reader almost physically back into the far past, a writer of whom I repeat, as I wrote in the *Sketch*, that he makes most of us who try to write novels feel that we should have taken up bricklaying.

He made one of his rare visits to London to attend a luncheon given for Martin Secker's seventieth birthday by those survivors of Secker's Young Men, as the novelists who emerged under his banner were known at the time when they and their publisher were promising youngsters—Compton Mackenzie, Frank Swinnerton, Hugh Walpole, Ivor Brown, Brett Young, Gilbert Cannan and Oliver Onions. (It is pleasant to know that now, twenty years later, Martin Secker himself, Swinnerton, Mackenzie* and Ivor Brown are still very much alive.)

I met Oliver Onions late in the afternoon after that luncheon and we talked till past midnight. He was a short sturdy man, bearded, good-humoured and very alert. He did not display his scholarship or behave like an important writer—indeed he hastened to tell me he was nothing of the sort. His modesty was matter-of-fact and utterly unboastful, though I felt that he quietly knew his value as a writer. He had been to the Hampstead flat where he had lived with Berta Ruck before the war and salvaged a few books, one of which, with incautious generosity, he gave me. It was a two-volume morocco-bound edition of the *Œuvres* of Frederic Mistral, inscribed by him *pour Monsieur Oliver Onions, de tout cœur F. Mistral, Maillane, Provence 29 Mars 1913* to which O.O. had added *From Oliver Onions to Rupert Croft-Cooke*. Mistral had been eighty-three years old when he inscribed the book and he died in the following year, six months before the outbreak of the 1914–18 war. Oliver Onions lived twelve years after he had made that

* Sir Compton Mackenzie died in November 1972

noble gift to me and in *A Send-Off* a short essay in *A Trickle of Welsh Blood* his wife, very movingly, describes the scattering of his ashes in the sea. 'I know it was a good-bye such as would have appealed to him. Evening sunlight on the sea, hills in the distance, men about him who, I think, esteemed him as a man and paid honour to him as an artist.'

Only when posterity has had time to—in the army phrase—sort them out, the bogus masterpieces and the quiet achievements of this age, will he come triumphantly into his own.

CHAPTER FIVE

Merry Hall and Taconeo

[1]

A MONTH or two after I had moved into the flat in Doughty Street, I drove down (no problem at all at that time) to see Beverley Nichols at the home he had bought at Ashtead in Surrey. I had known him for twenty years. We were poles apart in our views of our profession and in much else, but there had always been enough common ground between us to maintain a friendship full of laughter, and what we lacked in shared experiences and ambitions we made up for in our dislikes and forms of ridicule. We found the very persons of Godfrey Winn and Louis Golding, for instance, irresistibly funny and amused one another with stories of their latest gaffes and exploits, the cautious savings they had amassed and the absurd pretentiousness of both of them. But these were not the only topics of conversation we enjoyed.

Beverley had achieved brilliant success very early. President of the Oxford Union, he had published a public school novel, *Prelude*, while still in his teens, and in his early twenties made a great reputation for his portraits of celebrities which he published in the *Sketch* in 1925 under the title *Are They the Same at Home?* at the same time writing for the *Sunday Dispatch* those articles so neatly attuned to the time and place, *Freaks of Mayfair*. He wrote his first house-and-garden books and went round the world with Melba, using that experience to write his satirical novel, *Evensong*. Up to the outbreak of the last war he had continued to write and to *be* a considerable figure in the world, lightly and with humour touching on religion among the Moral Disarmers, then impertinently called Oxford Groupists, the dangers of war in *Cry Havoc*, and on other themes to which he dedicated all his original talents before he passed on to something altogether new. He was often sincere but seldom profound, a sort of super journalist, the liveliest columnist of the day. But in addition to this he had unusual social talents and marked discrimination in deciding whom he should cultivate. His house in Surrey at this time was filled with a great many people who were, or had been before the war, figures of note to the columnists, though scarcely any of them were writers. Beverley had never been 'literary' in the ugliest sense, and even when he had written about writers in his *Sketch* and *Sunday Dispatch* days it was as a very shrewd interviewer saw them and not as a fellow-writer. He thought—rightly I believe—that writers were never of much interest to the general public compared with film stars, artists, peeresses and prima donnas. So he himself was known to several hundred of the world's more spectacular characters as 'Beverley', a popular figure, a host, a gay companion, an eligible young man, a wit and someone met in the continental watering-places of the time, Le Touquet, Aix-les-Bains, Cannes, of whom his friends wondered how he 'found time to do his writing'.

I do not wish to seem to belittle his work, but it always appeared calculated to *épater le bourgeois*, or to light up his own originality, to reveal a new angle, to startle with an astonishing headline. Even when Beverley was writing in a cause very dear to him, he could not resist making its entertainment value his first consideration. Years ago, when I had achieved my first three novels, he had waved them aside with some characteristic advice. 'Go and interview Bernard Shaw,' he said. 'It's difficult but not impossible. That will show an editor what you can do.' But I did not want to interview Bernard Shaw or show an editor anything except perhaps an article written in my home, so the advice was never heeded.

But now in 1946 Beverley regarded me as being among his old friends and considered what progress I had made in my profession as sufficient to enable me to talk on equal terms with him of royalties and serial rights. Indeed he rather welcomed it; he knew very few professional writers. And when I went to see his house at Ashtead, appropriately named Merry Hall, he offered me the lease of a studio in his garden as a week-end resort and I gladly accepted it.

Merry Hall was a red brick Georgian house in a lane lined with trees, a fine house, a gentleman's manor, though it stood close to the road. It had more than an acre of garden, which nowadays would be viewed with disapproval by town planners as seven-eighths more than the accepted allowance for a whole family. Supported partly by his large salary for *Woman's Own*, for which paper he wrote a weekly article for more than twenty years, Beverley lived in it alone with his manservant who had served him for rather longer, and sought permission, difficult to come by in those years, to improve it or make minor additions. His was an enviable and highly civilized form of existence.

When he offered me the studio down the garden path I saw more possibilities than merely a break from London each week-end. It would mean that whether I liked it or not I should become acquainted with a large number of his friends and have to exercise social graces at which I was inexpert. I had never lost my good bourgeois ability to 'behave like a gentleman', in fact I sometimes wondered whether my upbringing had fitted me for anything else since I had eluded athleticism or even sportsmanship, and only after leaving home had learned to mix widely or to appreciate anything in art or architecture. But six years of entirely male company in the army, and years before that of circus folk and gypsies, had incapacitated me for the more elegant and flattering mannerisms needed for the bright exquisite stars of a quarter of a century ago.

Beverley grossly exaggerated as he pulled my leg about this, saying that I sat with my back to women and like certain cat-haters 'could not bear them in the house'. This was not of course true, but it took me some time to treat them as—absurd generalization—they like to be treated by men of my type, as male friends. However, as time went on and my tenancy of the studio lasted two or three years, I lost the shy diffidence that many men coming out of the Services felt, and I made friends, some of whom I have kept to this day. These were chiefly at the annual parties Beverley gave when his Regalia lilies, which filled a large area of the walled garden, were in bloom, and lovely clothes were worn and there was an atmosphere of a *fête pastorale*.

At one or another of these parties I met stars of stage and screen: Frances Day, incredibly youthful, who thought nothing of dancing all night and diving into a swimming bath in the early hours of the morning, more sincerely devoted to pleasure than the gay young people of the twenties, Walter Pidgeon who told me he had enjoyed making *Mrs Miniver* more than any other film and felt in no way out of place as an American in a film whose whole point was its Englishness, and Dickie Attenborough, then a somewhat podgy but very likeable young man who looked as though he had just come out of the school tuckshop.

Of writers I met few and they were not, for one reason or another, in the main stream; Michael Arlen, who had not published a novel for ten years and was not to do so again but was still a 'name'; '*The Green Hat: A Romance for a Few People* 152nd thousand' his publishers advertised once, and he was the first novelist to mention venereal disease as part of the theme of a novel or to use phrases such as 'her eyes were like spoonfuls of the Mediterranean' in his oddly affected prose. I found him charmingly modest and without the least pose or pretension.

Monica Dickens was a good-humoured somewhat talkative blonde whom one would never have supposed, either from her work or her appearance, to have been descended from Victorian Charles. She joined Beverley and me in writing one of three endings to a short story which started, as one of the Dolly Sisters was supposed to have done, with a penniless journey to Monte Carlo. It was not in the least my cup of tea but, when Beverley and I made a radio feature of it, he was at his best, brilliantly re-writing the whole thing in the Ivy before we were on the air, a dizzy but amusing and memorable occasion.

The producer was Reggie Smith, who claimed to be an orthodox communist but could never convince me that he was anything so unamiable. He and his wife, the novelist Olivia Manning, became good friends of mine long after the broadcast was forgotten.

The only other writer, if he can be classified as such, was Godfrey Winn, a very strange creature, a man of some talent as a master of the game of Bridge, a Wimbledon tennis player, an astute financier, a shameless exhibitionist, but none whatever as a writer. To see a letter of his or to read an article before it had been revised by one of the several friends whose job it was to make it presentable (as members of the editorial staff of the *Daily Mirror* had done when Godfrey first started writing about his mother, his cottage and his dog), was to realize how narrowly he had escaped complete illiteracy and to wonder at his accumulation and clever investment of a considerable fortune.

Godfrey was everything second-rate; gushing, hideously sentimental, a poseur whose highest ambition was to get himself into the presence of some member of the royal family, a non-writer, an expert in self-advertisement, and a bore. But he had those unexpected talents for tennis and Bridge, he could ingratiate himself with a great variety of people and he had a flair for money. 'At least he had a brave record in the war,' I said to Somerset Maugham, believing that the old man would be pleased at praise for his protegé. 'I often wonder whether it was bravery,' said Maugham acidly, 'or whether it was sheer c-camp.'

I saw a good deal of Godfrey during those years. He was anxious to consider that we were intimate friends and he gave me well-meant but patronizing write-ups in the women's magazine that employed him. But I found him unendurably shrill and silly.

[2]

More interesting were the people I met wandering across the lawn at one of Beverley's evening garden parties in summer, or in winter beside the log fire of the music-room. They were not connected with the stage or literature, at least not primarily; Ronald Howe,* for instance, the head of the CID who became, on retirement from the police, a multiple company director. He seemed a very approachable man so long as no attempt was made to draw him to talk his own shop, his presence in that *galère* accounted for by his friendship with Somerset Maugham. Then Gavin Faringdon† gentlest and most likeable of men with whom I established an enduring friendship, and 'Chips' Channon‡ with whom I decidedly did not, finding him chatty, socially pretentious and tiresome, the very man to be keeping that absurd diary which was published after his death and should have been suppressed for the sake of his past associates.

One of Beverley's parties was invaded by a group of undergraduates in tails. They were founding a magazine in Oxford and had come to ask Beverley to write for it. Most noticeable among them was a slim blond youth, Edward Montagu.§ I liked him at once and have continued to do so, not only for himself but for the supreme courage he has manifested.

A character of seemingly eighteenth-century magnificence and amplitude was Bob Boothby‖ whose conversation was lively with reminiscence and whose rumbling wit emerged from it when least expected. I did not see him from the time when he came down to Merry Hall till he arrived in Tangier ten years later and showed himself a mite puzzled by that curious watering-place. A splendid man of whose conversation, like Gilbert's oysters, I have never had enough.

*Sir Ronald Martin Howe, CVO, MC.   †Lord Faringdon.
‡The late Sir Henry Channon.   §Lord Montagu of Beaulieu.
‖Lord Boothby.

[3]

If I had been, even in this unlikely period of hob-nobbing with people of more or less noisy reputation, one of those novelists and general writers who believe that their true avocation is to write for the stage, who remain stage-struck to the end of their lives because someone has incautiously told them that they write good dialogues; if I had been the literary counterpart of the funny young man whose friends tell him that he 'ought to be on the stage', I would have considered the most important friendship I formed at Beverley's home was with Peter Daubeny and his wife Molly. I *do* think it was one of the happiest of such relationships, lasting as it has to this day, but not because I inevitably met through them a large number of screen and stage stars.

Indeed this was probably the worst way to meet them, surrounded by their co-professionals, when they were free to talk shop. I have grown in my life to dread the gushing phrases of theatrical shop more than any form of conversational torture and, although there are exceptions, most of even the highest in their profession never cease.

Ivor Novello, for instance, was frankly a bore not only to me but to anyone who was not prepared, for hours on end, to hear about his and other people's productions—a sad disablement for one who had once been the handsome Prince Charming of musical comedy. Some of the women, perhaps the best actresses, were not much better, but I would rather remember those who transcended staginess or were glorious people in spite of it.

The late Gertrude Lawrence, for one. By several freaks of chance we were thrown together—a most unsuitable association, one would have said, between a writer of forty-five with no interest in stage talk, and one of the most brilliant stars in the empyrean, the two having nothing in common but a love of humour touched with satire and a loathing for pretentiousness and second-rateness. Gertrude Lawrence was above all a friendly woman; she could release unexpectedly the most scathing remarks, but never to hurt unassuming people. She had, as everyone knows, a face in which this warm character was revealed, kind eyes and a seemingly innocent voice which never abandoned its gentleness but could voice the most devastating iconoclastic remarks.

I remember once Gertrude Lawrence came with Peter and Molly Daubeny to my flat for a late supper. I realized that one of the penalties of being a great star away from home is that (because hosts are anxious to do 'the right thing') she is forced to live on a diet of *pâté de foie gras*, expensive shellfish, caviare, smoked salmon, *cuisse de grenouilles*, avocado pears in Europe, venison, strawberries out of season and grouse. Though privately convinced that Gertrude Lawrence would have preferred some English childhood's favourite, I had not the courage not to conform. She appeared—what else could she do?—to enjoy this and afterwards offered to help Joseph wash up. I took this at first to be a form of affectation—star at the sink, I'm-not-at-all-grand-you-know—but catching her eye I realized that she really wanted to do it and gave her her own way. Joseph, who had intended, according to our custom, to leave the washing-up to the char in the morning, responded bravely and reported afterwards that Gertie Lawrence was in fact a competent and speedy washer-up. She was a most enchanting woman and when I met Noël Coward some years later I realized how much she had been appreciated in youth as well as in later years. Their correspondence was famous and if it is ever published will be seen as spontaneous. 'You see what comes of biting your nails!' wrote Coward on the back of a postcard reproduction of the Mona Lisa. I wonder which of the hardworking comedians of today's television is capable of throwing off that!

It was at the Daubenys' house, too, that I met Daphne du Maurier and drove her with Gertrude Lawrence from South Street to the Savoy in the unupholstered back seat of the Opel.

I had only been told two things about Daphne du Maurier, both, she hastened to tell me, totally untrue. It was *not* a fact that out of the eighty thousand pounds she was paid for the film rights of *Frenchman's Creek* the Inland Revenue collectors had left her less than two thousand, and it was even farther from the truth to say that she drove round London in a white Rolls Royce. In fact she lived a commonplace industrious life in Cornwall. Which only shows.

Then, central to any gossip column, which this chapter is becoming, were 'the two Hermiones'—not, I hasten to say, together for I believe they never were so, except on the stage—but on separate occasions in the Daubenys' home. Their superb comedy together, the hatred which according to popular rumour they bore one another apart, the exotic gifts of character which both of them possessed, the two voices with which every mimic familiarized himself, the kindness and yet the piquancy of both of them, they are memorable women who were never without a proud court of followers. It is good to have been on the earth for a short spell at the same time as the two Hermiones (Baddeley and Gingold, I need scarcely add) and I am grateful for it.

Perhaps the most interesting man I met in that hospitable house was C. B. Cochran, the great, the immortal C. B., who had dominated the theatrical West End of London for three generations and talked with youthfulness and *éclat* now when he was well into his seventies. My circus books were what interested him; we talked about the circus for long periods, during which he showed that he knew, unlike so many talkers on the subject, a great deal about it. But Cochran, at least as I knew him, talked refreshingly little stage shop and never mentioned his own scintillating record.

So that, with a few celebrated nonentities who even today appear in gossip paragraphs dragging their titles after them, these were the men and women I met at that time who seem worth remembering in this small catalogue. They led of course to other avenues noisy with the sound of names dropped on the driveway, but though I like comprehensiveness in writing these books, enough, I think, is enough.

[3]

But there was one occasion which was for me unique since I attempted dangerously to bring together the two ends of the extremes I explored and invited a party of gypsies to my flat to meet with a carefully selected party of men and women who had only humanity in common with them. The whole collection consisted of a number of talented and professional Spanish gypsy dancers, a group of illiterate tent and van-dwellers from the English counties, a few journalists and a number of theatrical celebrities and writers.

It was a foolhardy thing to do and nearly ended in violence, and it proved nothing at all except the fact, already known, that a few words are common to their respective vocabularies. But if it was a dangerous occasion, the danger flashed and glittered; if it served no serious purpose it made a few hours memorable to those who shared them.

The Spanish gypsies were distinguished people of a race which still holds manual work to be degrading. Work is for donkeys, say the Calés in Spain, and their occupation is to dance and sing. The ones who crowded into my flat that night did both of those things exceedingly well for the party consisted of Carmen Amaya and her formidable family. But the English Romanies have long fallen from their high estate. In the restricted and orderly life of a smaller country they have been forced to share common dole and to work now as field labourers. Their three representatives that night I had shanghaied from the pea-fields of Worcestershire where they had been picking for a week. Carmen Amaya was appearing then at the Prince's Theatre with a company entirely drawn from her own tribe. Her superb performance was almost as exhausting to the audience as to herself and one left the theatre always with a sense of being drained of emotion. Her spontaneous and barbaric *alegrias* have unpremeditated variations. One could watch her a hundred times following an ostensibly identical programme yet one saw each dance as though it were for the first time. She has the precious gift of never ceasing to create, however often she might perform. Her dances seemed to be the precise expression of her own moods which were never twice the same.

She was born in the caves of Granada. Before she was five years old she was dancing in the Albaicín and at the age of eight was appearing in Paris on the same programme as Raquel Millar. She was famous throughout Spain before she was sixteen; her songs had been recorded and she had danced in films. Towards the end of the Spanish Civil War she went to South America and toured it and Central America from Argentina to Mexico, surrounded always with her family. She was not twenty years old when she took them to the United States and had phenomenal success.

She remained a true gitana, unspoilt and little changed by circumstances so improbable to one of her race and lived in modern cities the free life of the Calé.

The suggestion came first from a theatrical press agent who took me to the theatre where I learnt from Carmen Amaya that she had heard that day that gypsies of a kind existed in England.

'Do they sing?' she asked.

I thought of my English Romani friends even at that moment breaking the peace of the night in many remote places as they shouted in their raucous penetrating voices the sentimental songs of thirty years ago.

'Very loudly,' I told Carmen.

'And dance?'

I remembered the hobbledehoy tap dances of the didakais which sometimes achieved real skill and brilliance but were more often noisy exhibitions to anger a protesting publican.

'After a fashion,' I replied. 'But our gypsies have not the gifts or distinctions of the Calé. They work in the fields . . .'

'They *work*?' said Carmen. She herself had just given a performance for which years of grinding labour had prepared her, but to hear of members of her race as agricultural workers was shocking to her.

'But they deal in horses,' I said loyally. 'They are to be found at race meetings and fairgrounds. The women still tell fortunes. They never do anything but piecework. They enjoy life, too. They . . .'

'Where can I find them?'

'It would be hard in London. And if there are any here they have settled in houses.'

'I would like to see some.'

'Then you shall,' I promised rashly. 'I will bring some to London for you. Will you come to my flat next Sunday?'

'May I bring my family?'

I had seen her family that evening form the *cuadro flamenco* for her *alegrais* sitting in a crescent on the stage and with guitars and *palmadas* accompanying her dance.

'Of course,' I said.

It left me with a truly difficult problem. I had promised her English gypsies and I was resolved that she should not be given mere didakais and costers from the London suburbs but people as nearly true Romani as our tans could produce. It seemed to me that my best chance of finding these would be in Worcestershire for I knew most of the families gathered there now. On the eve of the day arranged for Carmen's visit I drove down to Pershore determined not to return without my guests but knowing that I would need a glib tongue, great patience and determination, some obstinacy, much tact and endless ingenuity if I was to persuade two or three people of primitive habits who had never slept under a roof or seen a great city to leave their wagons and accompany me to London for two nights.

I needed more. I had to distinguish between real willingness and smiling assent given for the sake of politeness; I had to obtain a dozen promises that no power could prevent the speaker's attendance though I did not expect or need more than three of them to come; I had to explain away such problems as how the right railway station on the return journey could be distinguished by folk who could not read and had never been in a train; I had to perjure myself by showing that I would lose face, be 'in shame' for ever with my friends, if I returned to London with none of them. I was faced with situations such as the one which arose when my old friend George Lock wanted to come but could not because, he confided in me, his wife Nelly would 'never leave him alone afterwards'. Nelly repeatedly told me that George could go if he wanted, that she would *like* him to go; why didn't he? But George drew me aside to say—'You don't know her. She only *says* that.' And I had to satisfy parents and interested parties that no harm could possibly come to my guests and they would all be back on Monday night.

I had to leave Pershore by noon on Sunday to be sure of reaching London in time to prepare for the Amayas' visit that evening. And on Sunday morning there was not a gypsy in sight. The pubs in which they usually collected were empty, except for a few old people who felt secure against the most pressing invitation to London. None of the many who had promised without fail to meet me and accompany me were to be seen. Little Egypt was in hiding.

I had rather anticipated this shyness and did not even then abandon hope but began to drive out to the different leafy orchards and quiet woodsides where I knew their wagons stood. I listened to more ingenious excuses, including one from a Smith who told me there was a curse on any of his family who went to London and if he was to go he 'wouldn't never come back again alive'. But at last, unexpectedly, I suddenly filled the car with three daredevil adventurers for whom I had bought more liquor than was good for them.

I drove away as fast as I could. At every moment I expected to hear regrets from behind me, if not demands for an immediate return. Not until I was approaching Oxford did I feel at all secure in my capture.

The three I had, though, were worth all the trouble. There was the beautiful Renie Fletcher, quite the most handsome English gypsy girl I have ever seen, with a dark flushed face and a Burne-Jones aureole of dark loose hair. There was her swarthy brother Bill and there was young 'Nip', Neptune Loveridge, whom I had known since he was a ragged youngster of nine. The men wore the knotted scarf or diklo that would be expected of them and Renie wore the simplest green dress. We reached my flat an hour before the *gitanos* would arrive.

For that night I must use the bedraggled word fantastic, and the gypsies themselves were only a part of the fantasy. The English ones had no experience whatever of plumbing—or to be frank, not one had ever used a flush lavatory in his life. They had never talked to anyone but other gypsies, farmers, publicans and over-inquisitive policemen. They felt trapped and troubled before their ordeal began and only as the night progressed grew easy, and then too easy, as events showed. The Spanish ones, on the other hand, were over-civilized at first. Beautifully dressed and with the polished manners of cosmopolitan dancing stars, they seemed too polite to be natural. But this, too, wore off before very long.

Carmen's press agent had been at work and the first arrivals were a number of bad-tempered photographers, disgruntled at being sent out on a Sunday evening to what they clearly thought was a publicity stunt. Then came the Amaya family, disembarking from a cortège of taxis and trooping upstairs—no less than sixteen of them. They were charming to the three Romanies but a little perplexed and wary behind their good manners.

Soon after their arrival a number of incongruously sophisticated people made their appearance. Arnold Haskell who had written with enthusiasm about Carmen's dancing, Hermione Baddeley who was playing the Gypsy Queen in a review sketch,

Beverley Nichols who brought Carmen a great armful of Regalia lilies from his Surrey garden, Peter Daubeny who had not then emerged as a ballet impresario but was later to bring Rosario and Antonio to London.

There were incidents. Grandpapa Amaya had come with the rest of them, but kept aloof. He alone of them had always refused to make any compromise with the world into which Carmen had led her family, but remained a grand old primitive who remembered nostalgically his days of horse-dealing and nomadism. As a symbol of this, perhaps, he never, in any circumstances, removed his hat and sat now on a straight chair with his hard round hat pulled over his eyes and an expression of scornful disapproval on his face as he watched this drawing-room nonsense and longed for someone of his own mettle. Suddenly he rose to his feet and addressing the room announced *'Quiero miar!'* When I had been summoned to interpret I managed to lead the old gentleman out to relieve himself.

Then Renie Fletcher, who was drinking gin for the first time, lurched up to me beside Hermione Baddeley and said—'Tell the *rauni* I think she's beautiful.'

'That's very nice, dear,' retorted Hermione gamely, 'but it's hardly my *line*, if you know what I mean.'

Renie then announced that she was going to sing and began a sentimental ballad in a hoarse whining voice, only failing to finish it because she collapsed in a heap on the floor.

Carmen herself was inexhaustibly patient and charming. With no more than a few words of English she showed the good temper of a hard-pressed artist in satisfying the exigent demands of friends, pressmen and photographers. She even appeared to enjoy herself.

But presently I was called over to a corner where the two young English gypsies and Carmen's handsome cousin Antonio were gathered. Someone with quick perceptions had realized that there was danger here. The young men could not speak to one another, of course, for although there are plenty of words common to Romanes and Calo the gypsies in both England and

Spain now use so much of the language of the country and so little of their own that nothing like a conversation is possible between them. Fierce hostility had, however, grown up between the two groups. Each seemed to feel some challenge in the attitude of the other.

All gypsies love a fight and among the young men an evening's drinking is not considered really enjoyable unless there is one. Nip Loveridge was a notorious koring moosh and had been excluded from most of the pubs and dance halls in the area he travelled. Consciously or not he was looking for an occasion to show his skill and courage, or rather to be himself rather than the show-piece he felt was being made of him. The menace in his attitude had communicated itself to Antonio who, under his civilized clothes and manner, was no less spoiling for conflict.

As yet the two were sparring only with looks, or with words to those around them. Nip was telling Bill Fletcher what he would like to do with 'this lot whoever they were' while Antonio was confiding in another cousin that he could manage the two English gypsies alone.

As a temporary measure I interposed a couple of reporters who were delighted to find that Nip's real name was Neptune. Then I quickly explained the matter to Carmen who led Antonio into another room and introduced him to two girls who were instructed to keep him entertained. The party went on to a late finish without giving the young men another occasion to meet.

On the Monday evening the English gypsies went to the theatre to see the Spanish ones, and for their performance had nothing but passionate and tautological praise. They could dance, whatever else they could do, said Neptune ungrudgingly. A pity that there weren't English diddies who could dance like that, he added.

There had been, once. Not quite like that, since Carmen was unique, but dance and song were the common heritage of all gypsies and remain their only occupation in most countries.

They brought their music and dancing with them from India and the Indian origin of both is very plain today.

All that is called flamenco in Spain has been carelessly ascribed to 'Moorish influence', but the gypsies did not reach Spain until Moorish influence had passed its zenith. And what, one must ask, did it influence, what art had the *gitanos* in the Peninsula to *be* influenced by the Moors? The answer, of course, is that they had their own native arts with which they had made their way, dancing and singing across the world, from India.

It is impossible to hear the *taconeo*, the beat of the sole of the foot and tap of the heel with which a Spanish gypsy advances without remembering the Kathak dances, and the language of gesture in both is too close to be a coincidence. Moreover the tambourine, which has been seized on by the dancers of Spain and Italy, was a gypsy instrument with no counterpart among the Moors. It is the *gangira*, still used by Indian dancers, an instrument so old that it can be seen in the hands of stone-carved dancers in the oldest Hindu murals.

As for the music, there is the same endless improvisation, the same wailing voice, the same over-accentuated rhythm, the same spirit in Indian and flamenco music, and the curious should try the experiment of playing gramophone records of each alternately until, but for the differing instruments, it would be almost impossible to distinguish them.

It is seen, too, in the dancing of the gypsies in India, those descendants of the tribes who stayed behind when our Romanies' forefathers decided to travel westward. These so-called 'criminal tribes' move about in great bands and derive a part of their income from displays of dancing. They dance in far more abandoned fashion than the strict and formal temple dancers, quaffing quantities of country liquor or palm wine between dances and working up to wild and sensuous displays much as the Spanish gypsies do.

An expert could trace this farther, could follow each flamenco movement and gesture back through the centuries to an Indian temple. For when those hordes of fierce, pleasure-loving nomads came among us, bringing no literature and only a few faint racial memories of the past, calling themselves Egyptians or Bohemians or whatever suited them best, they brought something which they could never forget, their skill in music and dancing, and we still have not realized how greatly this has influenced our own. The negroes have not given so much to the New World of the tom-tom beat of Africa as the gypsies in Hungary, Spain and the Balkans have given to us of the plaintive and rhythmic music of India.

A few years after that to me memorable evening Carmen Amaya died, a tragedy for the theatre, for the gypsy race and for those who had known her.

CHAPTER SIX

Abroad

[1]

OF ALL the pleasures of 'before the war' which I remembered most nostalgically were those impulsive expeditions across the Channel which I had occasionally been able to afford to make, at first by train and on foot and later by car. They had become so remote and impossible during the last seven years that I gaped when I read that during the First World War, wealthy travellers wintered as they were accustomed to do in the South of France or even Egypt while the *abattoirs* of the trenches continued to thrive. True there had been a kind of travel possible in 1939–45; to the Americas for escapees or to various theatres of war for those in uniform, but it had, of course, lacked the liberation and ecstasy of driving oneself to any chosen place in Europe.

This, at the first possible moment, I resolved to do. To France I must have made at least a dozen journeys during the first five years of what was jokingly called peacetime, and most of them took me through Paris since it was still possible for any reasonably skilled motorist to drive about it.

I have realized one thing about this city—that it changes its whole ambience from year to year, almost from day to day. The Paris I first explored as a lonely boy when I was supposed to be a tutor to the son of a rich man living in Passy, the city I found so voluptuous in 1922, had disappeared when I visited the excitingly vicious and sophisticated Paris of the later 1930s, where I was assured, as I have recounted in *The Sound of Revelry*, that war could never touch Paris—'there may be an air-raid or two—nothing more. The Maginot Line is unbreachable.' Second-hand reports of Paris from my German friend who was among its occupying troops in 1940 gave me another and by no means shameful picture of the city, and now with the reactions of peace it had changed yet again. I could still drive about it, as I could about London, a feat now impossible at most hours of the day; I could still go shopping for food to take to England, for clothes and a few luxuries forbidden at home; I could still sit in cafés in Montmartre and on the South bank without being drilled in multitudinous packs among fellow tourists, and I could still eat magnificently at unprohibitive prices. The atmosphere was no longer the friendly generous one of before the war, and had in fact become somewhat suspicious and guarded, as well it might after years of occupation. The de Gaulle family—or was it the Daughters of the Revolution or a sinister combination of the two?—had closed the brothels and restricted all the more libidinous pursuits of Paris, but it was still a city to love for its liberalism and for its occasional urges towards the old gaiety, when vice had been commercialized, as by its very nature it must be, but remained elegant and scented.

But I never stayed longer than a week or two in Paris and, although at different times in my life I have believed I wanted to live in the city, there has always been some practical reason against it. If I added together all the short stays in my life in Paris they must total two years or more, but at this period I left it to dawdle for some hours in Versailles—to me then the most unspoilt of the seven wonders—and make my way southward to the winelands of Bordeaux and thence to the Landes.

I suppose the village of Roquefort (one of the five of that name in France) still exists. I will even concede that it has probably not greatly changed since the nineteen forties and fifties when my boyhood's friend Robert Cahiza lived there with his wife and two little sons not yet of school age, in a low ancient Landais house overlooking the hills and forests. But for me Roquefort is no more. I do not intend to be whimsical when I say that it has disappeared from the map of my cognizance. Robert has gone to live in Paris now among the tycoons of the great timber and papermaking firm of which he was then the local director, while of his small sons who toddled to the local school one is a married man and the other a successful doctor. The house, the long white house, the *potager* about it and the echoing dining-room in which we ate so well and drank *Armagnac* from a favourite cave not ten miles away, or Champagne, which the little boys called *poum*, from the *vignoble* of Robert's father-in-law at Epernay, has passed to other owners and Madame Coraillet, that wonderful witch-like little woman who produced such superb meals on the small stove in the general living-room of her inn, has died long ago and there are no ortolans such as she kept in aviaries at her back door for the needs of her customers. The village street has become a busy highway and the factory which Robert supervised spreads doubtless to unforeseeable dimensions. I have not returned to Roquefort for a decade and do not wish to do so again.

But in those summers I was a frequent guest and drove from Roquefort to Biarritz and Bayonne, and once to the incredible town of Pau, with its Boulevard des Pyrénees like an enormous balcony overlooking the mountains, and from there on to Lourdes where I prayed for miracles of healing which then seemed unnecessary. In the Casino at Pau on the night after my return from Lourdes I met a young English doctor and asked how he explained the many faithfully documented phenomena of the place.

'I can only tell you,' he said without expostulations of scepticism, 'that ailments, disabilities even, which have been hysterically induced—and who is to know which are so—can often be hysterically cured.'

It was a sensible and polite way of speaking but I still think the marvels of Lourdes are beyond such facile scientific explanations. I have, I think, good reason for doing so, for I have one of those stories about Lourdes which so many of us superstitious Catholics can recount. It tells how one day in

1926 my friend John Hitchcock, son of a Primitive Baptist and descendant of a line of fiercely bigoted Lutherans, was dying of rheumatic fever. This was when my father lived at a place in Kent called New Barn and the nearest Catholic church was a converted thatched barn two miles away at Hartley. Returning from a visit to it, I followed a footpath through an area of unbroken woodland, in those days unspoilt and almost unvisited, and unexpectedly met a small figure of which I like to recall, with a story-teller's exaggeration, that he seemed to pop up from the undergrowth. He was in fact a diminutive Catholic priest named Father Hoare; he was staying in Hartley and we walked along together. I told him what was on my mind, that my most intimate friend was in danger of dying, and he chuckled like a leprechaun.

'Don't worry about *that*,' he said, 'I leave tomorrow for Lourdes and will say a few prayers for him. We'll soon have him right.'

Forgive me for stressing the facts which go with a story like this. John *did* begin to recover just forty-eight hours later in a manner which one matter-of-fact doctor, who knew nothing of my encounter in Hartley woods, described as miraculous. What is more I never saw the tiny priest again, or discovered any facts about any Father Hoare staying in Hartley.

All right, so let's call it a coincidence, that favourite word of all sceptics. But at least it explains why the only queue I joined in those processional years that followed the war was the slow shuffling file which led to the grotto at Lourdes.

[2]

Once, before driving down to Roquefort, I spent a fortnight with Joseph in Normandy and Brittany, realizing that from the Indian view the differences between the countries of Europe grow less sharp—indeed tend to disappear. All their languages

ABROAD

being foreign, all their people being of sallow complexion compared to the rich beauty of the Eastern skin; all their shops and houses seeming very much alike to such a stranger to them, Joseph could not feel the tingle of excitement in crossing a frontier which from boyhood to this day has never failed me. We gambled at Trouville and stayed in a modest *auberge* at Fécamp, and found that in that year, 1947, so soon after the war there was scarcely more traffic on the roads of Brittany than when John Hitchcock and I had walked from Caen to St Malo in 1926.

There was a little incident which seems to me now to have presaged, though in a trivial way, some of the sorrows and frustrations of the frontiers, walls, alarms and migrations which were to come. We crossed the Channel uneventfully with the Opel on the Townsend Ferry and were passing through the Customs when Joseph on demand produced his passport—a British Indian one.

'You need a visa,' said a brisk official.

My British passport was all right; Joseph's being issued in Delhi was not. What was more, the official would not stretch a point to enable Joseph to have a fortnight's holiday in France. The AA Scout, other passengers, I and Joseph himself pleaded vociferously. Nothing could be done about it.

Now this was before immigrants from the Commonwealth had come to England in great numbers. Joseph was in fact among the calculably small number who had arrived since the war. But there it was. He returned on the same ferry to Dover, rushed up to London, obtained a French visa and crossed again while I waited twenty-four hours in the dreary country round Calais, anxious and expensive hours for both of us. The immigration official earned those words which became so commonly applied to all such little bureaucrats in the years ahead—he was *within his rights*.

[3]

Those were the years in which I really came to know France, not as a perpetually surprised and impressed visitor as I had been before the war when I had found wonders in each new area from the Basque country, with its churches in which the sexes were separated and the pretty painted boats jumping on the harbour of St Jean de Luz, the Vieux Port of Marseilles and the beaches of the Côte d'Azur, the mountains and lakes of Grenoble and Aix-les-Bain, the glory and gold of Provence and the Burgundian vineyards up to Strasbourg and the roof-nesting storks of Alsace, always feeling that I was travelling, learning, finding experience, always aware that I was a privileged explorer. That had been an apprenticeship to Gallicism, but now that I was becoming at home in a country which showed little outward sign of the recent occupation, but had certain other characteristics in common with England, I felt that I was almost an inhabitant. I knew the long Napoleonic roads on which it was never possible to be far from good food and drink, where every village offered its temptations to the traveller who glanced at his Michelin Guide, *curiosités a voir*, *monument interessant*, *bonne table*, *vins locaux*—it was hard to pass them by.

Motoring in France for an Englishman was not as before the war something of an adventure when one's car was hoisted on to the ferry boat by a crane and one stopped at night in a roadside hotel to find a small group of English holiday-makers at the bar discussing the chances of travel and the performances of their cars. Nowadays, even so soon after the war, it was all taken for granted, the furious driving of the French, the white veal which the English had not tasted since 1939, the tart retorts which were made instead of the warm courtesy of pre-war France. I loved the country no less than I had done since boyhood, and the people only a little, though I recognized that never again should we, the English with our omnipotent pound (of which we had once needed so few to live royally in France), be welcomed with ingratiating smiles but now were treated with formal civility by people of ostentatious independence. France had not changed, only the whole tribe of *hôteliers* and those who depended on foreigners for their living—the people, in other words, most in evidence to the visitor had changed irrecoverably. It is worth remembering that this change had come about before the vast invasions of the Continent by package tourists.

[4]

The French, between whom and the English there must always be a kind of love-hate relationship as there has been throughout history, were not the only people I wanted to visit with the new emancipation that had come to me with civilian life. There was an area of Europe of which I had no personal knowledge, partly because the journey I made in 1937 to write a book called *The Man in Europe Street* had not included the countries which were embraced by it—Denmark, Sweden and Norway. Deciding to do something to remedy this I found that travel through them by car was still comparatively inexpensive and easily achieved, and I booked a passage from Harwich to Esbjerg for myself and the Opel.

Denmark seemed to me to thrive, almost to exist, on two literary traditions, *Hamlet* and the *Fairy Tales* of Hans Christian Andersen. If Shakespeare had not decided to make a play out of Kyd's crude old melodrama and created the magical word Elsinore for its setting, there would have been little to distinguish the kingdom of Denmark from other seigniorial estates during the centuries of its preoccupation with agriculture and terrible little wars. If Andersen had not written *The Little Mermaid* as inspiration for a sentimental sculpture on a rock in Copenhagen harbour, there might have been almost nothing to recommend it to enquiring minds then, and little today but its trade in dairy produce and pornography. There was Andersen's birthplace at Odense, a rather grand eighteenth-century house as I remember it, an unlikely place of business for the working cobbler who was Andersen's father. For me there was also at that time bountiful food after the sparseness of England, there was a literary agent who had sold translation rights of some work of mine, and in Copenhagen there were the delights of a pleasure garden called the Tivoli at the very centre of the busy commercial city. I found the narrow lanes called Strøget which twist out on to an open square where you may see the copper roofs which have turned green with verdigris, and I was invited to some restaurants round the fishing port where the fish and shellfish were supremely good. But after that I crossed the ferry to Sweden and followed my impeccable AA route (supplied so promptly in those days) and made my way up the beautiful coast of Sweden through cities whose very names I have forgotten and among incidents blurred into a summer happiness of blond and beautiful young people on bicycles and on foot, the youths showing their torsos to the brief intense sunlight and the girls with plaited ropes of ash-blonde hair.

I must have passed through Halsinborg and Halmstadt, Falkenberg and Verberg and perhaps stayed the night in one or another of them, while Göteborg is scarcely memorable to me except as a commercial port in which I stayed in a rather grand hotel. So I made for the Norwegian frontier.

It was there that my adaptability as a driver finally failed me. I had started driving on the left of the road in England, crossed Denmark holding to the right, had found myself once again (in those days) on the left in Sweden and finally on the right in Norway. In a moment of absent-mindedness near Halden I had that nightmare experience which may have troubled the dreams of other motorists, in the centre of the road with a large car approaching and myself for a dizzy second unable to remember which way I should turn the steering-wheel to avoid it. Whichever I did was wrong and the big car with a scream of brakes managed to miss me by going into the ditch on the wrong side of the road.

I ran to apologize to a solemn and visibly shaken magnate whose chauffeur had saved his life and mine, also to help get the car out of the ditch. The magnate, as I supposed him to be, spoke in English unsmilingly. 'Nothing to worry. We are both safe. What more can we ask? It was a mishap. Motoring is dangerous to all of us.'

It was with relief, some years later, that I learned that after a referendum Sweden had decided to conform to the custom of the rest of Europe and now its drivers keep to the right.

[5]

Norway was a very different place for me. If I had been born under another flag it would have been the Norwegian that I should have chosen. Not that I knew—or know today—very much about its traditions or history but names and places and people have captivated me from the time when I learned Kipling by heart in my preparatory school. Names particularly, Bergen, Spitzbergen, Harald Haarfager, the Vikings, Olaf, Haakon, the Fjords, the Skagerrak and later Narvik. When I taught in a school in Argentina a Norwegian merchant sailor named Hoy, had sent his three sons with cropped yellow hair, blue eyes and powerful small bodies to learn with the Anglo-Argentine boys from whom they stood out in character as much as appearance. Then, like any growing intelligence in my early twenties I became enthusiastic about Ibsen and for a period thought Greig, though not in his mediocre *Peer Gynt*, to be a very great composer.

But there had been a more recent conversion to Norway of a more practical, even gainful kind—a Norwegian publisher had chosen books of mine for translation and had sold them in surprising quantities. Most English writers have acquired a reputation in one particular European country often out of proportion to his success at home. (I remember, for instance, finding that in Czechoslovakia the name in all English letters which acquired most prestige was that of a novelist named Claud Houghton.) It was typical of my commercial bad luck, I used to say, that I had been chosen by a country with little more than three million inhabitants, and although presumably in isolated farm houses with flowers growing out of the peat roofs they spent the Arctic night in reading, this could never be much of a source of income to me.

But it gave me a friend in the publisher Per Mortensen who showed me the enchanting city and took me by ship to one of the islands on which he had a châlet, a memorable August day of sunlight and laughing water and lobsters and good talk. Per also introduced me to his father who had built up his publishing business through having virtually a monopoly of Correspondence Courses which Norwegians took seriously.

The elder Mortensen had an amiable idiosyncrasy. In his magnificent flat, furnished with articles cleverly designed from the timbers of his country, he took me with pride to a bar stocked, he claimed, with supplies of every liquor known to man. You had only to choose a *saki*, an Indian palm toddy, a Madeira Velhisima, bottled perhaps in the time of Napoleon I, a *cognac* of such age that its potency was gone and all that was left was sentiment, a poteen from the West of Ireland, and old Mortensen chuckled with pleasure. What he wanted was a challenge and it was rarely that he could not meet it.

Oslo is a city which more than any other I know in Europe shows a respect, a positive love, for the past and for the symbols of its own history. This has been supposed by some critics to suggest its decadence in modern times—to these I should suggest a visit spent in observation of the Norwegians themselves, than whom no less decadent race exists. But they have made special buildings to house Nansen's exploring ship *Fram*, and three original Viking ships in a wonderful state of preservation, while in their extraordinary Folk museum they have re-constructed typical early dwellings. They have a sense of the past and a reverence for it, not a maudlin longing to return to it for all its greatness, such as you find in North America.

Clearly I can only speak of Norway as a summer tourist whose whole stay in the country did not last more than a fortnight. But I know what part of Scandinavia I should choose as a home, and that without having seen the touristical wonders, the *fjords*, the midnight sun or the infinity of pine-covered hills running down to bright blue water.

[6]

The weather was clouded as I made my way back through Stockholm, and perhaps because of this it seemed to me that no Swede ever smiled; certainly none ever laughed outright. It was of course a delusion; there must be frivolous, gay, happy Swedish people but it grew on me that as hours went on I could not find any signs of it. Waiters solemnly brought you food, barmen stolidly poured your drinks, even the people on the beaches knew no joy in the sunlight or the surf, while as for business men, representatives of my literary agents, they invited me dutifully to dine or lunch with them without the least apparent pleasure. A publishing firm, named portentously Natur och Kultur, had published (by mistake I could only suppose) a light-hearted novel of mine, *Ladies Gay*, and I went to the large offices of the firm to call on their managing director, who received me with ritual politeness but seemed to think that we met to bury the book not to find any humour in it.

The city of Stockholm has been called—though modern Swedes seem not to find the name quite respectable—the Venice of the North. It has a certain beauty but the inhabitants seem unaware of it, their minds being bent on other matters more to the point than attractive surroundings. Perhaps it is their restrictive licensing laws, or perhaps they remember even in summer the harsh winter they have passed or the snowbound one ahead, or perhaps they are naturally taciturn people. In the nightclubs, even those frequented by homosexuals, assignations were carefully made—and no doubt would be carried out punctiliously. I did not unfortunately visit a cinema or a theatre but I pity Swedish comedians working in the atmosphere of a crematorium without even the spooky irreverence of a churchyard.

I have met Swedes who practised the conventional use of laughter but they were—now I come to think of it—expatriate. The Wachtmeisters in Paris whom I described in *The Glittering Pastures*, and two carefree young blonds called Stefan and Arne who ran a bar in Tangier; they all seemed to be intimidated by the thought of their own homeland.

[7]

I can scarcely count among these journeys, tame and European though they seem to be, one I made to Northern Ireland. A member of one of the important cotton-spinning families had been among those luckless individuals who had 'failed the course' in Field Security, and had spent the rest of the war in some menial work at the depot. I had known him there and when he asked me to stay at his home outside Belfast I accepted in order to write the last chapters of my novel *Wilkie* away from the distractions of London.

The experience was not without absurdity. The house had been built by my host's late mother some thirty years earlier. It was called Windy Brow, which says almost all there is to say, and it was surrounded by a garden of the kind one often finds round the homes of the rich in the home counties, carefully placed rocks, masses of aubretia, tarmac paths and tidy little lawns.

Since I went in 1947 I was surprised if not impressed by the luxury hotel atmosphere, central heating and plentiful supplies of servants, wireless receivers not only in every bedroom but in the bathroom attached to each bedroom as well, six-dish breakfasts duly kept ready on hot-plates for late-comers, a Rolls Royce to be brought round by a chauffeur and dangerously thick new carpets over every scrap of floor-board. My host showed me a large collection of modern manufactured jewellery and invited me to borrow anything I wanted to wear and drink of course was unlimited. None of these would have been so exceptional ten years earlier or ten years ahead, but in the first days after a war in which civilians had suffered privations, it seemed unbelievably vulgar. However, I should have been more grateful. I worked in my large warm bedroom—stationery and stamps supplied—came down to sumptuous meals and finished off my novel in very little time. I saw little of Northern Ireland except the hilly views from the windows of Windy Brow which were, I must own, superb.

CHAPTER SEVEN

The Wheatsheaf

[1]

THE ONLY chronicler of the nineteen-forties who made something distinctive of that extraordinary period, part war-time, part blundering peace, all change, surprise and anomaly, was called Julian Maclaren-Ross, an unusual young man who lived through the fifties, 'a decade which I could well have done without', as he called it, and died in 1965. This Maclaren-Ross became for a short time a familiar part of my London life as he did for many other people—he saw to that. You couldn't just be vaguely acquainted with him, you might find his pretensions intolerable or you might be amused in a friendly way, but he was difficult to ignore once you had come within his orbit. And make no mistake about it—he *had* an orbit. He sat every night at a certain place at the end of the counter of a pub called the Wheatsheaf, a few yards from the Fitzroy, and he was never alone. He succeeded in persuading a number of people to crowd round the tall stool on which he sat, dressed winter and summer in a teddy-bear coat which had once been smart and cosy-looking, but was now what is called, in this case accurately, a shadow of its former self. He carried a gold-topped malacca cane which never left him and he talked in a loud good-humoured voice of things about which he was enthusiastic or knowing.

He was not a good conversationalist or raconteur—how could he be with such shameless exhibitionism? But one found oneself near the end of the bar, fascinated by his patronizing good will to all around him and wondering what he would tell

THE WHEATSHEAF

his listeners next. That stool at the corner, for instance, was not just a preference of his; it was a necessity, and tales were told of him hurrying in at six o'clock to secure it, or sending stool-sitters in advance to hold it for him. If by chance he was too late and feared it might be occupied, he did not come into the Wheatsheaf that night at all, rather than be forced to take another place.

In appearance he was tall and at that time round twenty-seven or thirty. He had a face fairly well modelled but from an unhealthy-looking clay.

His career was a fairly conventional one for a writer. He had lived impecuniously before the war selling vacuum cleaners, canvassing, anything but labouring or professional thieving, until he was called up for army service and this, instead of killing any talent he may have had, released a flood of quite brilliant short stories of army life which were published by *Horizon* and other periodicals and afterwards appeared in book form. Young writers either begin with poetry or with short stories, and sometimes both, but Julian's stories were remarkable for their maturity, innocent-seeming humour and finish, and they made him quite a reputation in the years before I knew him. I would not say this went to his head for he wanted to talk far more about himself than his work, but at this time, about 1947, he began a barren period which lasted well into the 1950s, being apparently too satisfied with himself to write any more. Meanwhile he quarrelled with most of the editors and publishers who had befriended him, promised to deliver manuscripts and neglected to do so, listened to the siren voices of phoney film producers and generally sank to devices to raise a pound or two at which he seemed fairly successful because several young women, whom he treated badly, always seemed around to keep him alive. He had one lovable quality, or was it only a flattering one? He talked enthusiastically about his friends, building up their meagre or supposed qualities to brave proportions. Soon after I met him he heard from someone absurd Munchausen stories about me, that I had boxed for my school—totally untrue—and had taken the island of Madagascar almost single-handed. He listened to my ridicule of both fables, but preferred to believe his informant and thereafter forced his hearers at the Wheatsheaf to pretend at least to credit him which led to some embarrassment. Of others he preached other fables; a Singhalese emigrant called Tambimuttu, owned in his country, Julian had heard from a girl named Kitty of Bloomsbury, an estate in Ceylon called Tambimuttu Towers. Julian afterwards spoke with some awe about the scrubby little man, while Julian's heroes among literary men and women were innumerable. He afterwards wrote of them with salt, even with a touch of satire, but in conversation he found them irreproachable and worthy of his praise—Anna Wickham, Calder-Marshall, G. S. Marlowe, Moray Maclaren, Val Gielgud, Woodrow Wyatt, and even more obscure figures who were trying to emerge as writers or editors at that time, though soon after many of them grew tired of work and disappeared into the more restful occupation of commerce.

If I mention other people under the heading of Julian Maclaren-Ross, I do not mean to infer that I met them in every case through his introduction, though many of them I did; rather that from the evenings I spent at the Wheatsheaf, or at the Fitzroy, or with those I met there, I came to know a section of people naturally related to Julian and his pub, or at least so they appear in my memory, people very different from other writers and artists I knew, people to whom may be applied a long series of epithets, Grub Street scribblers, bohemians, amateurs, charlatans, and a few genuine hard-working writers some of whom have achieved fame in the years since then.

There was, for instance, a young ex-naval Haileyburian called Alan Ross. He was clean-shaven then though he afterwards grew a beard, perhaps to conceal the outline of his long questing nose. I met him actually with Julian and invited him to spend a week-end with me. He seemed half public schoolboy, guardedly enthusiastic, half protégé of John Lehmann with an assumed sophistication, but in all aspects a friendly, interesting young man who gave me a grandly produced quarto book of prose sketches of Corsica with a few poems, illustrated by John Minton, dedicated to Roy and Kate Fuller and published by John Lehmann. It was all rather twee and each of the poems had a dedication—to Julian and Kathleen Symons, to Alan Pryce-Jones and so on.

That week-end was a memorable one, for in the afternoon on Sunday we decided to swap introductions and as both the victims lived in Hamilton Terrace it would be easy. Mine was Louis Golding, with whom I happened to be on speaking terms at that time; his were the artists John Minton and Keith Vaughan across the road.

Mine was the greater failure. Louis worked like a beaver, as he always did to impress younger men, and rather wretchedly failed. He could not avoid an element of patronage as from a best-selling writer to a tyro even when he talked about Corsica which he had known some years earlier, and he pretended, in his usual way, that he had run out of spirits of any kind and offered us Cypriot sherry.

It was I who was the failure at the home of Minton and Vaughan, for I regarded a huge wall-length panel of John Minton's as a piece of extended book-illustration and thought poor John, who committed suicide a year or two later, a giggling, superior young man and made very little contact with Vaughan. I'm sure now that John Minton's giggle was a nervous one and that he was a devoted and sometimes inspired illustrator. An hour or two of Louis Golding must have exhausted me and I behaved boorishly at the joint home of Minton and Vaughan—like that of Ricketts and Shannon half a century earlier. However Alan Ross seemed quite pleased with the whole occasion and I felt that it had, though rather meaninglessly, enlarged my ambience.

After that week-end I do not remember ever seeing Alan Ross again, though I have a disturbed memory of a phantasmagoric party of John Lehmann's at which Alan Ross appeared in a beard and with the girl he afterwards married—phantasmagoric because in half-waking memories a lot more things return to me which may not have happened. Did Roy Fuller appear in matelot's rig having just been released? It seems scarcely possible today. I'm pretty sure I fell out with Julian Symons (A. J. A.'s brother) and I distinctly remember telling the wife of Edward Hyams that her husband couldn't write, and I dare say I was guilty of other gaffes. A pity, that. But I console myself by knowing that whatever that particular circle say in conversation or in print of my books, I can live by writing them, and that is all I want, or have ever wanted, to secure. It means the supreme happiness of being able to live by doing what I want to do most, and doing it as well as I can.

[2]

To return to Julian Maclaren-Ross and the people I met directly or indirectly through him. After I had known him for a month or so there dawned on me suddenly the realization of what the whole pose and costume meant. Somebody must have told him that he looked like Oscar Wilde, and the coat, the cane, the plummy voice, the tallness, the complexion and the longing to *preside* over his friends, certainly bore this out. How he must have longed for a fur coat in order to replace the old teddy bear, and how he must have searched for an occasional epigram, or even a witticism to enliven the rather commonplace material of his talk. But all this added to my enjoyment of Julian's attitudinizing and I liked him no less for it.

I used to set out in the evening in the Opel, which had stood all day outside the flat in Doughty Street, then drive along to cross the Tottenham Court Road and disappear into the streets of that portion of Soho which lay north of Oxford Street and was sometimes called Fitzrovia. I could leave my car without difficulty anywhere there I liked, outside the Wheatsheaf or the Fitzroy or one of the Indian or Cypriot restaurants which abounded there. Then I would make for the Wheatsheaf, wondering who would be there. Nina Hamnett, perhaps, who never cadged drinks however much she was in need but when given one would respond with stories of long-ago characters whom she had known—and she had known pretty well everyone. But Nina was only for certain evenings when one felt able to listen to her endless catalogue of curious more than famous names. She had the vice of connecting everyone she talked to with someone else. She once told me that she had known certain friends at Oxford of my brother Lawrie, and every time I met her after that she would speak of Leonard Bower, Jim Tovey, Arthur Walters-Welsh or Graham Eyres-Monsell, names that never meant much to me and now meant nothing at all, recalling old scandals and incidents in which she expected me to be deeply interested. She had been a brilliant artist in her day, she was among the frequenters, described by Augustus John, of the Eiffel Tower restaurant in the great days of Rudolf Stulik; she was mentioned in countless books of reminiscences by countless autobiographers, always in different and startling connections, including her finding the body of a girl in the Crowley/Neuburg thaumaturgical set who had shot herself through the head. She had known Gaudier-Brzeska and almost every artist in Paris and had more recently been described by Arthur Calder-Marshall—'with her long thin legs and her cloche hat streaking like a busy emu from the Fitzroy to the Marquis of Granby'. She seemed immortal and remained recognizable from Gaudier's day to ours, and although she became an alcoholic and a wastrel, enough mental energy was left to make her a 'character'.

Another odd character who hung round Julian was a man then called Peter Brooke about whom I wrote in *The Wintry Sea*. He afterwards changed his name to Anthony Carson and when I first heard this name it did not occur to me that this was a pen-name chosen by an author in preference to his own, indeed I felt some sympathy with a man branded with this novelettish name.

He talked of 'experience' as though it were a commodity in which he had invested, of which he now held a large stock ready to be put on the market.

'What kind of experience?' persisted his questioner.

Mostly his experience as a courier to a travel agency, it appeared, but there were other things. He had a lot of experience.

Nearly everyone who came to the Wheatsheaf in those days had an inkling that he himself and the rest of us were somewhat laughable figures, even Julian Maclaren-Ross, even one of Freud's grandsons—not the painter but a young man in publishing. Even Dylan Thomas, drunk or sober. Even the young men who did unrecognizable sketches of the customers at half a crown a time. But not Peter Brooke. He could see nothing funny in himself, or in not being able to get his work published when it was so full of experience, and nothing at all funny in having a perpetually unassuaged appetite.

'This novel of mine . . .' he would say, bringing the conversation back to the point at which he had left it. I volunteered to read the novel at last, for at the Wheatsheaf we were all a little tired of it. I found it sound solid stuff about a heroic courier to a travel agency and the situations he came up against. Whatever was funny in the book it was not the travel agent's courier. He was a mesmeric man, brimming with experience, not at all a man to laugh at.

It seemed just the book for the literary agent who acted for me then and I introduced Peter Brooke to him. I was not mistaken. It was promptly placed with one of the Hutchinson companies. But it did not sell and Peter Brooke's manner to me grew rather reproachful afterwards. His stock of experience had been expended in vain.

[3]

I met Dylan Thomas at the Wheatsheaf but not through Maclaren-Ross. He came in with a very ancient and rather infirm-looking Augustus John and they remained very pointedly at the far end of the bar, which surprised me because Julian had often talked about his friendship with Dylan a year or two earlier.

They were both rather drunk though John should, as they say, have known better—he was well over seventy and looked older, his eyes wide and hollow and his whole frame supported by a heavy stick. He knew me from a temporary association with a body called the Gypsy Lore Society, of which he was president, and introduced Thomas, though I felt pretty un-Welsh between the two of them. Dylan, as was his custom when he found himself not—for a few minutes—included in any discussion, began to improvise lines of rhythmic prose about gypsies of whom he knew nothing, with mounting oratory but not much sense. John had no respect for this; he wanted to talk about the gypsies he knew, and did so, driving Dylan to further verbal excesses, louder and louder, declaiming about a bucolic uncle of his, a good subject for rhetoric as Smollett and others have found. Thus the occasion became something of a shouting match, John talking about Esmeralda Lock and her marriage to the Town Clerk of Bridgnorth and her running away with the romantic lexicographer, Arthur Hindes Groome, and Dylan discussing his probably imaginary uncle.

John looked somewhat gaunt and hollow-cheeked at this time, like an old French master gone to seed, not venerable but aged, boozy, and autocratic. Perhaps he had made a sentimental journey to dine at the Tour Eiffel as he had once been in the habit of doing and Dylan had steered him round to this pub. I never knew the circumstances but I do know that I wanted to hear John talk about gypsies and found Dylan with his grandiloquence about his uncle to be rather tedious though admittedly inspired—or so most of his devotees would have thought.

I never saw Augustus John again though we corresponded several times. But Dylan I saw once more in less unfavourable circumstances. I went to see Louis Golding late one evening and found Dylan there. I will not say speechless because I gather he was never without speech, but very, very drunk. Among the many biographers who have written about Dylan there are those who complain that others who speak of him on slight acquaintance always emphasize his alcoholism, but I feel no shame in this. I only spoke with him twice and on both occasions he had what Wilde used to call poetically 'vine-leaves in his hair'. It is possible that earlier biographers of poets, of Keats, Shelley or Byron for instance, may have noticed the same thing but were too discreet in their nineteenth-century way to say so. Now we are less restricted—or mannerly.

When I came into the room at Louis Golding's there was something more than this in the situation, for Dylan turned his back on Louis and, without recognizing me, addressed me exclusively during one of his long declamatory speeches, half poetry, half obscene prose. What was strange was that Louis appeared indifferent to this neglect; he was busy hunting through his shelves. Dylan went on, conversationally, almost affectionately, ostraboggulously, as Victor Neuburg his first discoverer called it, and made some sense as his poems make some sense. I began to enjoy myself. Dylan, I discovered, was a talented entertainer when I had not John to listen to; he stared with unseeing eyes into mine and his talk, his oratorical talk, went on unceasingly. For the first time I realized that I was listening to a remarkable, a unique soliloquy, something that no other human being, drunk or sober, could have produced. Among all the biographers and 'intimate friends' there have been no imitators or parodists, no one who has attempted to mimic Dylan in full spate. He was unique.

But suddenly he was chilled to silence. Louis had achieved the purpose on which he had been engaged. He had at least half a dozen books in front of him—all Dylan's or anthologies containing work of Dylan's.

'I want you to sign these, if you will, Dylan. I should be so pleased. Yes they're all yours. Here is a pen. Would you sit down there?'

And Dylan, scarcely knowing what he did, wrote rude words in all of them while Louis almost guided his hand. Louis did not mind how rude they were. They had become 'Association Copies' as the book-sellers say. He beamed with joy then led the way into the open air before Dylan could consume any more liquor.

[4]

I do not know where I met John Morris but the meeting was connected with some of these people and places and I remember on that occasion sitting with a bottle of whisky between us till the small hours. He was a man of remarkable achievements of which no parade was ever made and unless one turned him up in *Who's Who* one would never have guessed that he was MA, MSc. (diploma in Anthropology), had fought in the First World War in France, Belgium, Palestine, Afghanistan, Wazinistan and the N.W. Frontier, had been a member of two Everest Expeditions (1922 and 1936), had been awarded a medal from the Royal Geographical Society for explorations in Chinese Turkestan, and had gained many other distinctions in places as far apart as Cambridge and Tokyo and was now head of Far Eastern Services of the BBC. He had been an officer in that very Gurkha Regiment, the 3rd Queen Alexandra's Own, in which I had been commissioned during the war. He was not a frivolous talker, far from it, but I found him absorbing. He was an intimate friend of Morgan Foster's but filled me with no keen ambitions to meet that crusty old character, whose books I considered, though almost model novels of the period, were overrated and over-polished.

But John Morris was a great man and if he'd lived eighty

years earlier would have ranked with Burton whom he in some respects—though not physically—resembled.

He asked me to participate, on his Far Eastern programme, in a discussion on poetry with Roy Fuller, and this I did with great enjoyment though I would shudder to hear it played back today.

Another writer who had come to some prominence during the war, and whose short stories I admired immensely in a collection called *Something Terrible, Something Lovely*, was William Sansom, whom I used to meet at Bertorelli's Italian Restaurant, where before the war in hard times I could buy a plate of spaghetti for tenpence but now was a respected Soho restaurant with a loyal clientèle. Sansom was somewhat remote but that which so many of his contemporaries were not—a true professional; a mark of this being that he talked very rarely about his writing.

Yet another of the same generation though on rather a larger scale was Gerald Kersh. He seems to me to be one of the two potentially classic writers who had been seduced by film-making and have never achieved the books they should have, Gerald Kersh and John Collier. In their early books they seemed capable of illimitable achievement; their later, though never mediocre, did not seem the result of the progression they promised.

At that time Kersh was living at an inn near Ellen Terry's cottage in East Kent and I drove down from London to meet him and his charming Canadian wife and found him good company, modest and unliterary.

During this period I reached my final exasperation (as all his friends did sooner or later) with Louis Golding. It was a complicated matter concerned with some Jugo-Slav wine he was selling to me as a great Louisian favour when all wine was scarce, and discovered that he had been unable to resist making a profit on the deal. I had remained Louis's friend far longer than others, but this broke my resolution. It was a relief but a loss of entertainment too. Louis was absurd perhaps, egotistical and devious, but I had known him for twenty years and had laughed with him almost as much as at him.

The truth was that after the war, which he spent in America, he was never the same man who had amused and caused to wonder a number of friends; he was never again so entertaining or so companionable. The acquaintances he cultivated for their interest to him as a writer came from the new London breed of deserters, inhabitants of blitzed sights, petty thieves, service men on the make, lay-abouts whom even Louis could not idealize. They were tawdry and loutish and Louis failed to inspire in them the devotion which, he seriously believed, his pre-war cockneys had felt for him. He married an old friend from his own Magnolia Street, but even his wedding did not pass without absurdity. The two elderly people, both ponderously pot-bellied, received their guests at the Café Royal in one of their banqueting halls which had been booked for a later occasion by a famous dance-band leader, whose guests began to infiltrate before Louis and Annie had come down from the throne, in which they had sat side by side throughout. There was an embarrassing tangle of clashing personalities.

Not long afterwards Louis died, followed within a few weeks by Annie. I lived in Tangier at that time and had long ago dropped all acquaintance with him, but the report I received in Morocco was to the effect that poor Louis's funeral was even funnier than his wedding. How cruel people are, but you can't, as they say, help laughing.

One of his less lovable characteristics was a noisy contempt for people whose names were confusable with his own. I have recalled in *The Numbers Came* an occasion when he greeted me with laughter which only an expert in Louisian tactics would have recognized as forced.

'What do you think this silly ass had done?' he said, indicating an article in one of the intellectual weeklies. 'Confused me with Douglas Goldring!' He laughed again but with a glance at me to make sure that I enjoyed the joke.

I did not. I knew Douglas Goldring, who was a friend and

biographer of James Elroy Flecker. He was anything but a showy writer, or a showy man for that matter, but he loved letters, had a quiet reputation and was much respected by young writers who used to see him at the Fitzroy Tavern.

'I don't see anything wrong with that,' I said rather huffily. Louis's laughter became more forced.

'You have so little sense of humour,' he replied. 'Me, with Douglas Goldring! It's rich! Douglas Goldring! Oh my giddy aunt!' The laugh died rather abruptly. 'You're very obtuse sometimes,' he said severely. But now he was sorely tried for there had arisen a writer named Goldman, and another who would soon make it impossible for Louis to dismiss him as an upstart—William Golding who wrote *Lord of the Flies*. I did not see Louis by the time that appeared but I should have liked to watch his reactions.

[5]

I had two publishers after my escape from Walter Hutchinson and neither was a happy association—Macdonalds and afterwards Werner Laurie. I decided to accept an offer on very solid terms from a very solid firm—Macmillans, for their history went back for more than a century of distinguished literature. There was a great deal of flap and brouhaha about this and the firm in a very mannerly even distinguished way gave it to be understood that a candidate for Macmillans' list was greatly privileged.

Their offices then were in a little road off Leicester Square, something between a government department and a cinema foyer displaying portraits of the great stars, in Macmillans' case literary, such as Tennyson or Kingsley. Or more prominently Hughie Walpole beaming down with immense satisfaction. A commissionaire in uniform manned the door and a hush and importance prevailed in the hallway and panelled staircase.

There was in the building a directors' dining room and it was part of the ritual that an author joining Macmillans' should be asked for lunch at which the men of the family should appear, in those days Daniel Macmillan, the Chairman, Harold Macmillan, who as it afterwards seemed to me was spending too much time on the affairs of the nation to sell my books, and Maurice his son. It was the custom to ask some writer of distinction, not necessarily connected with the firm, to meet the newcomer, and in my case I was lucky for it was V. S. Pritchett, an amiable man. Harold Macmillan was then the Secretary for Air and had, I was told, 'just come across from the House' for this luncheon. This was a splendid welcome and although I cannot claim that I walked on air afterwards, down the wide staircase between the portraits of Victorian authors, I felt a certain security about the future publication of my work. Alas, things were not what they seemed. Macmillans are doubtless a great firm of publishers, just the people for C. P. Snow who joined them shortly afterwards, but with my lighter-hearted fiction they failed miserably and after six books, each of which sold less than the last, I felt that my sales would sink to nothing if I did not descend that magnificent staircase for the last time. But that was five years later.

Another commotion, one concerning copyright, cropped up at this time. I contracted to write for a firm called Sampson Low a book about gypsies, which now forms one of this series—*The Moon in My Pocket*. There were a number of photographs and when the book was published a man who had asked me to introduce him to my gypsy friends in Pershore in 1940 claimed that one or two were snaps which he had actually taken. At first I thought he was being facetious for we had both taken and exchanged photographs of the gypsies, but it appeared that he was in earnest, produced negatives and wanted credit for his two snaps.

Fortunately I was insured against this sort of thing and the company settled the matter at no loss to me. What was the idea I wondered and wonder to this day. Was he desperate to have his name printed in a book or did he really think there would be some damages payable, or what? But other writers tell me they have had to face odd situations like this in the course of their professional lives and are just as much at a loss as I was to discover a motive.

All these incidents I recounted to Julian Maclaren-Ross, when we were not playing *Spoof* at the Wheatsheaf, and he could generally cap them with incidents in his curious life of selling vacuum cleaners and short stories, learning the effrontery to face housewives at their doors in order to be able to face editors in their offices. He was particularly pleased with my introduction to Macmillans and created a sort of saga to commemorate it, for he had a ready eye for the preposterous. I do not know how often I went to the Wheatsheaf during the time I was living in London; it must have run into hundreds over the years, for it became a habit.

Even when I was a very young writer I wanted to keep a finger in each pie and went often to Charles Lahr's bookshop and other haunts of the literary bums and charlatans and some good writers, while at the same time keeping up my annual visit to Galsworthy, or occasional talks with Chesterton or other important persons. I did the same now but not, I think, as a matter of conscious principle. I liked both parties.

CHAPTER EIGHT

Round the Peninsula

[1]

IN THE summer following my little journey to Scandinavia I decided to return to a country which had in a sense been a second home to me—Spain. The very name now strikes a chill into those who had known it as a beautiful, rather backward and exciting country, in which the people one met were Spaniards and not masses of holiday-making British demanding fish and chip shops, or Germans who complained of too much garlic in the *fiambres* and not enough draught beer, or even French, with families of six crowded into each mini car. I am going to be a thorough snob about this and say that I detest most of my fellow-countrymen on holiday, especially in Spain, whole coastal areas of which they have turned into seaside slums.

I had been closely aware of its history since the nineteen-twenties, had known it in the time of Alfonso XIII when the contrast between its rich and poor was alarming, then in the era of the Republic when it was even more so, visited it briefly during the tragic Civil War with no wish to take part (there was altogether too much publicity-seeking as well as some heroism demonstrated by Englishmen in that), and now I wanted to see what had come to Spain under Franco, sure that it would be a very foreign country, still poor but not *so* poor. So I tried to return to another pre-war joy, and booked a passage on one of the passenger-carrying cargo boats of the Mac Andrew Line. This was asking for it. Did I really suppose that the £10 passage (no increase if the ship took more time) I booked home from Barcelona in 1932 on a ship called the *Ponzano* (Captain Gould) would repeat its joys for me at this time? Did I imagine that the travellers, who in pre-war days came because they needed or wanted to travel and not for a sight-seeing holiday, would resemble those who would be with me now? Cargo boats which do not carry a doctor are limited to twelve passengers so that one's enjoyment of the journey is conditioned inevitably by the eleven human beings travelling with oneself. I was willing to chance it, for whatever they were like they could not prevent me going back to Spain, approaching its cities from the sea, finding some familiar things and many new.

The *Palomares* was a smart ship, almost, as someone said, a private yacht for the directors of the company. The cruise—I must use the word with its ghastly modern connotations—was expected to call at a dozen ports, starting at Bilbao, reaching Barcelona and returning with calls at Cadiz and Portuguese ports. It cost if I am correct rather less than £50 the round trip and far from the little saloon which was all there had been on the *Ponzano* for meals and sitting space for passengers and officers (but what splendid conversations we had there!) the *Palomares* had an elegant dining saloon and a small 'drawing room', all polished and upholstered and absurd.

The voyage started well, since Captain Gould of the *Ponzano*, then semi-retired as passenger manager, came down to the ship and I had a long nostalgic conversation with that salty and humorous man. But it was with some anxiety that I examined my fellow passengers on the first evening aboard. They seemed harmless enough. A retired ship's captain and his wife having a busman's holiday, an orange importer and his wife travelling to Valencia on business, a 'lady novelist' who wrote romantic fiction for Walter Hutchinson with her engineer husband, and another couple who left no mark or sound on my memory, of whom I cannot recall whether they were old, young, tall or short, or where they sat in the dining saloon.

With the cheerful lack of *savoir faire* which seems to belong to ship's officers and shipping company officials they had set the Hutchinson lady novelist opposite me at the four-seated First

Officer's table instead of surrounding us both with other passengers at the larger more anonymous table. 'Two writers,' they had thought delightedly; '*they'll* get on together.' They had not an idea what a dangerous chance they were taking or that two writers on a small ship should be regarded as dynamite and be kept apart, whoever they were, or if possible locked in solitary confinement. They should certainly not be put facing one another for every meal.

It started badly. Mrs Durban mentioned that she had been recommended to make the voyage by 'her publishers, Messrs Hutchinson', and slipped in the fact that her sales exceeded twelve thousand copies. This was a totally untrue statement but it was not the lady's fault. Hutchinsons at that period, before Walter had committed suicide (and not since, it should be emphasized), used to print the most extravagant figures in their books '125th thousand' or 'sixty-first edition'. This was all right until one of the authors wrote, as I did, for the considerable sum in royalties that this represented on which Hutchinson had to confess that these figures were 'a matter of policy' and did not represent his system of book-keeping. So Mrs Durban who under her own name, or under a pen-name which I have unfortunately forgotten, probably sold as few as I did, and was, through some curious self-persuasion, buoyed up by the startling figures in her books. I suppose she was a sensible enough woman not to go too closely into figures. Her books were printed and advertised and this was enough to distinguish her from her friends who made no such pretensions.

However, on every subject except her books she was sane and I liked her husband so that before we reached Bilbao, a city I had never visited, I agreed to go ashore with them to interpret and guide. It was a notable fact that no one on that ship, not even the Captain or the orange importer, spoke more than three words of Spanish, a disability which had consequences later. And I was among the vast majority of English visitors to Spain, before and since, who have never visited Bilbao, a city of great distinction as I was to find ashore. We went to the old town and saw the famous seven streets, the Siete Calles which were one of the earliest of restricted areas, its paved streets being closed to horsemen and wheeled traffic in the fifteenth century, four or five hundred years before we learned to keep streets free of motors, a practice which I pray may be increased throughout the world until motorists are only permitted to drive on roads created specially for them. 'Their cleanliness,' it was said of the Seven Streets in that early period of preventing pollution, 'was the wonder of all visitors.' And so, in a different way, is the cleanliness and neatness and brightness of all Bilbao today.

It was while we were in the Old Town, I recollect, that we began to feel hungry and the Durbans suggested that I should find a place for lunch. 'Isn't there a big hotel or a famous restaurant?' they asked. I dare say there was, only I was unable to find it. I asked a man in the street and in the Spanish or Basque way he gave his whole generous attention to the matter.

'I will take you to So-and-So's,' he said, using a polysyllabic Basque name. 'It is not grand,' he said. 'But you will get good food.'

He started to lead the way and I watched the dismay on the Durbans' faces. At last he led us proudly through a bar whose floor was littered with prawn-heads, between a crowd of workmen and into an inner room where the *señora* said she would prepare a table for us.

The Durbans were now beyond all hope. They did not complain, for retreat without an unpleasant fuss was impossible, but it was clear that they thought I had betrayed them. However, an excellent if improvised meal was produced after about ten minutes. Three omelettes—and the Spaniards to my mind are the only omelette-makers who can compete with the French—then a little shape of *Arroz a la Valenciana* and finally a very simple chicken stew *pollo guisado a la casera*. I do not know whether my friends were more relieved than delighted. But on board they described the restaurant I had taken them to with enthusiasm, it was 'typical' and 'truly Basque'.

I was more impressed by the general aspect of Bilbao, less

than ten years after the Civil War. I expected to find it still torn with the results of artillery fire and bombing, embittered and frugal. There was no sign whatever of the war and all the tragedies, the ghastly massacres of Nationalist prisoners of war by the Republicans, the long period when it seemed that the city would be protected by its Ring of Iron, and the final days in 1937 when Franco's forces broke in and took possession of Bilbao. No city, one might suppose, would have been more scarred in appearance and in the minds of the people than Bilbao, yet here its inhabitants were smiling and friendly and well-clad. What was more, I began to be convinced on that first day in Bilbao of a fact which afterwards became familiar and certain—Franco had done that impossible thing, created a Spanish middle class. No longer as in every visit to Spain in the past did I suffer from the sight of very rich and very poor Spaniards; now between the two extremes, which were not so obvious, there were the vast masses of fathers and mothers and rather overdressed children who sat outside cafés and doubtless made the Sunday *paseo*, competing in new clothes with their neighbours. As a connoisseur of the picturesque you might not have approved of this, might even have remarked on the spoilt behaviour and noisiness of the children and wondered how a café proprietor could afford on Sunday afternoon to find all his tables occupied with family parties drinking one orange-ade every two or three hours, but as a human being you would be glad of it.

[2]

Our second stop, if I may use so unnautical a term, was Gibraltar and at this date when the Franco Government did not yet feel itself strong enough to demand its possession it was a friendly place. Its most useful function for me and many other British visitors was to provide clothes and groceries, both unrationed there, which could be paid for with money unrestricted in London banks by travel allowance. I purchased two suits—six years in the army had cured me of having clothes made to measure—and from Liptons a supply of essential groceries to be posted every month to London.

Then on the south-eastern coast of Spain we called at Dernia, a little port celebrated by Rose Macaulay where I sat at a café table in the main street explaining to the Durbans the beneficent habit of providing *tapas*—in those days without charge—with whatever drink one ordered. The coming of a few million English tourists has cured the Spaniards of such wasteful carelessness, and only in rustic unfrequented places are they still served without charge and as a matter of course. I had miniature *calamares en su tinta*, the little ink-fish which are tinned in Spain and Portugal and nowhere else in the world. Their appearance made the Durbans shudder.

Barcelona, the port of farthest distance from England (by the sea route), seemed to be little changed from the city in which I had lived for eight months in 1932, in 'the time of the Republic'. The Plaza Cataluña had not yet become a car-park and along the west side of it still ran an arcade of pillars and sheltered cafés. And although the Café Criollo and most of the brothels had been swept away by war or reform, the Barrio Chino still existed as an archaeological curiosity rather than as a centre of amusing and criminal vice in which Genet had been pointed out to me in what could only be called his natural state.

It was in Barcelona where I had first been taught to watch bullfighting and learned to see it not as a spectacular display full of sorrow and fear nor yet as a 'sport', which it is not, but as the dangerous art of killing bulls cleanly and if possible painlessly. Marcial Lalanda and Domingo Ortega were the great fighters of those days and I saw both and several others. Now as I returned to Barcelona the noble days of Manolete were over and since we had a Sunday in the port I was promised one of the popular bullfighters of the time—Antonio Caro, who was coming to Barcelona that week-end.

ROUND THE PENINSULA

I went alone to the Plaza Monumentál. 'No thank you,' said the other passengers and one could scarcely blame them. If I had not become used to the *corrida* in my twenties I doubt if I should have cared for it later, or that it would have become a part of the Spain I have loved for so many years. I saw Antonio Caro and cheered myself hoarse because it was one of his 'great days' when he collected ears and tails like souvenirs and was carried shoulder high through the city thereafter. At least I imagine that it was his great day for on subsequent visits to Spain no one seemed to think much of him or remember such a triumph as that one in 1947.

[3]

We left Barcelona to run South without calling till we should reach Cadiz. But after three days out, there was a singular event which had some effect on future events in my life.

There were four of us sitting in the little saloon, sometimes called the drawing room. I was facing the port-hole and the Durbans and the Captain had their backs to it. It was nearing midnight and we were thinking of turning in—all set in fact for a Conrad short story—when I was startled to see a face at the port-hole. One cannot trace one's reaction precisely on such an occasion; I knew it was not one of the crew though I cannot tell how I knew for I scarcely saw the features. Three days from port and out of sight of land, it gave me what they call a turn.

The face disappeared immediately. I said to the Captain—'You've got a stowaway on board.'

'Nonsense,' said Captain Evans. 'The whole ship was searched before we left Barcelona. It always is.'

'Well, he looked in at the port-hole just now. He must be on deck.'

I led the others, who were still sceptical, out on deck and as

I did so I saw a movement, a mere shadow, but something disappearing into the darkness under the companionway to the upper deck.

The Captain still believed I had imagined the whole incident and left me to investigate. In a moment I pulled out of the darkness, like an angler with something on his line, a boy of about seventeen.

'Ask him where he's been,' said the Captain, who as I have explained, did not speak Spanish.

'You'll do nothing of the kind,' said the only woman among us, Mrs Durban. 'Can't you see he's starving? Give him something to eat before you question him.'

It was she herself who found the tired all-purpose steward who looked after us and obtained a plate of thick sandwiches. The stowaway sat on the deck and, when the food came, indicated that he needed to wash his hands.

This touched Mrs Durban.

'Oh look! Before he'll even touch his food he wants to wash! Let him use our bathroom, Captain, please.'

The Captain appeared to think that the whole thing had gone out of his hands and shrugged. If passengers wanted their bathroom messed up by a dirty young law-breaker, he seemed to say, let it be on their own heads.

The stowaway was so long absent that I was asked to see what had happened to him. I found the bathroom full of steam and amidst it a naked young Spaniard choosing a large bath-towel from the rack. I told him to hurry up and in due time he appeared clean and fresh-looking and out of a smiling face one saw a pair of startingly cornflower-coloured eyes. He settled down to eat and waited respectfully to be questioned.

'How long have you been on board?' I asked him.

'Since we left Barcelona.'

'How did you get on? Where did you hide?'

'At night. I have been in one of the life-boats.'

It was I who was blamed, illogically but understandably because by this time I was considered responsible for him, for the fact that he had eaten some of the emergency rations which all ships' life-boats carry. But in the meantime I went on with my questioning.

'What is your name?'

'José Ricardo Moreno Iglesias,' he said.

'Well, Pepe, what made you do this?'

His face changed dramatically and well-prepared tears came into his eyes. He began a long spiel of confused lamentation. He had been persecuted as a Government supporter. (The war had been over nine years.) He was treated cruelly at home particularly by his mother. (She was a kindly materfamilias as I came to know later.) He was starved and beaten and his only hope was to get to England. (He was an habitual *polizón* and had already stowed away on the ships of three other nations.) Finally God and the Blesséd Virgin would bless me if I protected him now. I told him to stop all that nonsense. He was no more an anti-Franquista than I was and he didn't look in *any* way bullied. He was out for the adventure, that was all.

'It's a damned nuisance,' said the Captain. 'I shall have to report it to the Authorities in Cadiz and it may cause us to be delayed. Until then he must work.'

He was put in a small cell intended for port policemen to sleep in when they had to spend the night on board. I saw him several times during the next few days, always radiantly cheerful, the least persecuted teenager I had ever seen.

'What do you think will happen to you in Cadiz?' I asked.

'The police, of course.'

I told him I would try to get him off the ship and went to the Captain with a suggestion. I knew the two young apprentices by this time and asked them if they and some of their friends would walk off the ship with Pepe, since he could pass as one of the crew and with any luck would not be stopped. The Captain was enough of a gambler to take the risk. It would certainly save him a lot of trouble if it did come off.

As it did. Dressed in some bits of English clothes, surrounded by young members of the crew, he passed straight through the port gates. With a little money subscribed by the Durbans and a few pesetas from me he left on the Madrid train that night while I sat in the Plaza San Juan de Dios delighted to find that the large succulent prawns I remembered eating on my last visit to Cadiz were still offered for sale from baskets outside the cafés. (They have disappeared now I believe—all being canned for export to the United States.)

But there is more of the story of Pepe which I shall tell in its place.

[4]

Cadiz has always been to me a place apart, as though the isthmus beyond which it stands, with only a single road and railroad to connect it with the mainland, made it for me a separate country, as though there was Spain and there was Cadiz. Jocosae Gades, the Romans called it, and although there is nothing left of the city they built, a city renowned for its cookery and girls, there is something mysteriously Roman perceptible there. Visigoths and Moors held it for long periods and in the sixteenth century it was sacked by the British. After that it was rebuilt and its chess-board of lofty streets and its mighty walls enabled it to resist three other British attacks and can be seen in part to this day, including the magnificent fortified arch through which one enters the city from the isthmus road.

'Cadiz,' I wrote in *The Purple Streak*, 'like Venice and Rio de Janeiro, should be approached from the sea if the full impact of its beauty is to strike the visitor. It rises most gloriously from the water, its dreamlike buildings clustered round the golden-yellow dome of its baroque cathedral.' So I found it on this second visit and on my third, six years later, I lived there for a whole summer in one of the ghastly villas which have grown up on the land developed outside the walls, consoled against

ROUND THE PENINSULA

my immediate surroundings by the sea on one hand and Cadiz itself with its elegant cool streets and highly civilized people, welcoming one after entering through the great arch.

This time I lounged for long hours in the plaza where *cocheros* with flyblown cabs and horses still plied for hire, bought a sack of rice and a dozen bottles of Spanish brandy to bring triumphantly home, and was taken by the apprentices to drink in one of the several uninviting brothels which had not yet been abolished through the insidiously dirty-minded influence of American mommas who bullied their political husbands into persuading certain weak-minded European nations into 'cleaning them up'. The red lights are going out all over Europe, we noticed a few years later, and still hold the Daughters of the American Revolution responsible for this insanitary act of vandalism. I wish them joy of their call girls and midnight cowboys.

We made only one more call, at Setúbal, a few miles south of Lisbon, where I found the 'Portuguese Lord Jim' whom I described in *The Purple Streak* when I met him fifteen years earlier. He told me that he had developed tuberculosis now and as he also had a wife and four children I realized that his adolescent dreams of adventuring round the world were forgotten.

I also found, another relic of the past, that back street where prisoners in the local gaol were allowed to beg through an iron grille between their filthy common cell and the pavement. Passers-by looked in on them with curiosity and sometimes charity—a common sight, I dare say, of the Peninsula in previous centuries but one surprising to come on in 1947.

Then, without calling at Lisbon we 'butted up the Channel' for London docks. The steward gave me certain instructions about the importation of my brandy which proved useful.

'You see,' he said, 'the Spanish distillers of Fundador put on their labels *Fine Champagne*.'

I could not believe in this pretentiousness. Fine Champagne is the name of the locality in the Charente (cognac) district and is classified officially as the first of them all. It has, of course, nothing to do with the sparkling wine of Champagne which comes from the Epernay region. To name a Spanish brandy Fine Champagne was absurd. Yet at this time, as the steward showed me on the label of one of my bottles, Domecq, the makers of Fundador, the brandy I had bought, used it. (They have long realized its silliness and dropped it from their label.)

'What you want to do,' said the steward, 'is to declare your case as a dozen bottles of Champagne. Sparkling wine costs a bit more than others but nothing like so much as spirits.'

'But won't they know from the shape of the bottles?'

'Well, none of them has yet,' said the steward significantly, and I braced myself for my insolent deception.

'All right. Fine Champagne,' said the Customs man and I paid 8/– a bottle.

So I was pleased with Messrs Domecq's ridiculous labelling. I was not so pleased a few years later when I found that at the behest of their London representative a member of the publishing firm of Putnam had actually inserted, after I had passed the proofs of my book *Sherry*, a passage recommending Domecq's which I had not written or seen and could not endorse if only because I had never given any such puff to any other firm: 'Domecq's also, of course, is one of the largest and most important sherry shippers. In its long history, it has been granted three royal warrants by British reigning monarchs. *La Ina*, for those who like their Finos not too dry, is one of its most popular brands and, I understand, is a favourite in Palace circles. *Delicia* is a very fine dry Amontillado.' I have never before or since had words put under my signature by a publisher's assistant and I supposed that the only remedy when I discovered it, was to seek an injunction. In this case the managing director of the firm at that time was a friend, Roger Lubbock, and he was as much shocked as I was, so I let it go. But I remember it now with reminiscent anger. I believe this sort of thing is quite frequent in America, but in England, fortunately, there is a decent respect for the words the author has written. I could never be guilty in discussing brands of Sherry of the snobbery and Americanese of warrants from Queen Elizabeth II and 'a favourite in Palace circles'. It is a little late to put the record straight now, but I say here that these six lines were slipped in, after I had passed the text, by a man named John Huntington, a nephew of the original founder of the firm, who admitted the fact to me and Roger Lubbock. His motives I leave to the imagination.

But the brandy lasted a couple of months and enlivened my flat in Doughty Street.

CHAPTER NINE

A Collection of Episodes

I LIVED five years in the flat in Doughty Street, the longest I have ever spent in one city except Tangier, and even there I moved from one house to another during my stay. Doughty Street became very much a home for Joseph and me and we were both a little proud (why not?) when *Homes and Gardens* produced a feature about it with photographs of every room. Another feature was published by an Indian magazine the *Onlooker* for which we cooked an Indian meal, invited a dancer named Ram Gopal and squatting with him around a variety of Indian dishes, looked up to a camera. A tired old gimmick today when there is a take-away curry shop at the corner of every street, but quite startling then under the title *Little India in London*.

During our years in the house we had in succession three 'dailies' working for us, all obtained without difficulty by putting the same advertisement in the window of a local newsagent: 'Daily help needed for bachelor flat in Doughty Street.' This stressing of *bachelor* was a secret I had learned from someone wise in what used to be called the servant shortage, unspeakable words after the war. It appeared that 'Chars' will do anything but work under the supervision, or interference as they call it, of a woman and, although Joseph was a keener observer than any housewife, they accepted his admonitions which were always introduced with his friendly smile. There was Mrs S., Mrs C., and the Sergeant. Mrs S. was industrious, rather serious and somehow suggested an air of doom in spite of her polite smile. A year or two after she had begun working for us, and with all the domestic clichés, had 'got used to our ways' and 'never left a spot undusted', her bodeful manner was explained. She rang us up one morning to say with restrained hysteria that she had arrived home yesterday to find her husband hanging from a beam.

Mrs C. was next, a rather more interesting if less dramatic person, she was plump, red-cheeked, cheerful, in appearance a Victorian fictional farmer's wife. She got down to work with cheerful familiarity but explained that in common with her husband and son, she was a Socialist and 'took no interest in anything to do with the Royal Family and all that'; for she didn't, she explained, 'believe in it'. As the Socialism she claimed was limited to a dislike of anything to do with Royalty it seemed a rather one-sided form of idealism chiefly held, I thought, in loyalty to her family. How Mrs C. would have loved all the radio exhilarations over the Queen when she was crowned if only she could have followed her natural inclinations! She did not at all agree that giving independence to India was 'a good thing'. She wasn't very fond of Attlee or Bevin or Bevan or Stafford Cripps or Hugh Dalton, and looked rather crestfallen when any of them were mentioned, but she *had* got it into her head that Socialism meant abusing the Royal Family and enjoyed that as richly as a character named Hamilton appears to do today. She was a kindly soul and used a vacuum cleaner with the best of them. She left us because her husband died suddenly.

Our last was the Sergeant. She had held that rank in the ATS, and although she was no loud-voiced martinet she was dedicated to a kind of efficiency, a thoroughness, a positive affection for hard work that quite terrified us. 'I want this room now,' she would say when I had just got down to writing in my study. There was nothing to do but 'leave her to it'.

She remained with us for two years until we moved down to the country, and I have told the wistful story of her departure in *The Life for Me* but will repeat the main points of it now to complete our trio of housekeepers. It did not involve the familiar widowing of Mrs S. and Mrs C. It was in a way more macabre and inevitable.

It happened like this. There were some rooms beyond the kitchen of our new house at Ticehurst and I thought they would make admirable quarters for the Sergeant. She would have her own front door and a minute square of garden between her sitting-room window and Church Lane, the quiet little road which ran behind my house. Moreover, the bedroom had windows looking in three directions, one of which commanded the view southwards. A bath was put into the back room downstairs. She would have, in fact, an independent cottage with a way through to my rooms. This convenient arrangement had seemed to be one of the main advantages of the house. When I decided to leave London she said without hesitation that she would like to keep house for me in the country. It was therefore for her, for this domestic functionary whom even Mrs Beeton could scarcely have criticized, that the little cottage beyond the kitchen had been furnished, decorated and arranged.

'In fact,' said the Sergeant, 'I've always wanted to get back to the country. I shall never really be used to London. I'm glad you've decided to move.'

Merrily she did the work of three moving-men as we prepared to leave London, then drove down with me and Joseph to Ticehurst. We arrived on a warm August evening, and for the first time she saw the house and her own adjoining cottage. Her enthusiasm was loud and sincere. She saw at once where she would put her saucepans, her brooms, her cleaning materials. She seemed almost instantly to have settled in. She particularly approved of her cottage.

On one of the occasions on which the previous owner had joined me in examining the house and planning its adaptation we had looked into this housekeeper's cottage.

'This,' he said with suspicious casualness, 'was the mortuary.'

'The *what*?'

'The mortuary. Most village builders are undertakers as well. It's not often they have a corpse on their hands, but they have to have somewhere to put it when it does happen. They used this little sitting-room downstairs.'

We went out to the yard, and I never gave the matter another thought. After all, death must have occurred in most of the rooms of a house of any age, and past history of such premises is of little account. 'Mortuary' was a cold and ugly word, but the sunny little sitting-room with its window facing south had nothing in the least gruesome about it; indeed, like the rest of the house it had a friendly and contented atmosphere. The Sergeant, for instance, said she felt at home in it at once. Its past was forgotten as much as that of the rest of the house. But not, it appeared, in the village of Ticehurst, where people still shuddered at the thought of it.

'I shouldn't care to go into it at night,' one might say.

'Not very *nice*, is it?' another would suggest, while the name 'mortuary' is retained with a certain unction. Perhaps in all the century and more during which my house was inhabited by builders this cottage may have kept a dead guest for the night on half a dozen occasions, but there was the name, the forbidding and awesome name. I was up against one of the greatest powers on earth, that of words.

Had I guessed that anyone would give more attention to the matter than I did, had I realized that the people of the village still shivered and nudged at the mention of it, I should have warned the Sergeant. But I did not. What was more, there were local men still working in the house when we moved in, local people coming to the back door curious to see what strangely courageous stranger had made a sitting-room of the unmentionable apartment, and local shopkeepers serving the Sergeant and eager to discuss the grim matter with her. And on the fifth morning after our arrival at Ticehurst I came down to find no breakfast laid, a stillness in the kitchen and in the rooms beyond, and a note on the mantelpiece addressed to Joseph and stating simply that her luggage would be called for. A word, as potent as a witch's spell, had been breathed into her ear, and the angelic Sergeant had vanished.

[2]

But that was much later and meanwhile I had no thought of leaving Doughty Street in spite of the ever-flushing lavatory below and the motor coaches that pulled up outside so that the occupants could see the house in which Charles Dickens had once lived.

During my father's thirty-eight years of married life we occupied houses to which my parents moved their furniture on twelve occasions and the list of our homes sounds like a broadcast of train stops—Edenbridge, Lindfield, Chipstead, Tonbridge, Eastbourne, Hastings, Forest Hill, Orpington, Longfield, Hildenborough, Aldeby, Smarden, where my father died, by no means exhausted but looking out for yet another 'perfect little place'.

Doughty Street was only the eighth home by the same test I had occupied, Rochester, London W2, Barcelona, Wrotham, Salperton, Smarden, London W1, and London WC2, though if by the rules of the game I was allowed to count wartime places here and abroad each of six months or over I could add another half a dozen. Of my eight homes Doughty Street was the most eventful and peopled, though not the most adventurous. Something in the social sense happened every day, and for six years I enjoyed myself.

For instance there were friends from the army who came to the flat, friends whose names will be familiar to readers of *The Licentious Soldiery*—Julyan Pickering, 'Sergeant' Ede with whom I had tramped with others round the hills outside Glasgow, Senèque who had shared RP duty with me at Winchester, Arthur Pearce who had spent his Christmas leave with me in Zululand, Ohana who had been with me in Madagascar, Joe Power the ex-Commando, Stewart Hamilton, the ex-Marine, Peter Noble my host on leave in London, all of whom found me out and dropped in to talk—quite literally and sentimentally —of old times.

But I spent a great deal of time away from the flat for there was the week-end studio 'down the garden path' and many week-ends in my own Kent, finding out gypsy friends and publicans, and going to visit just over the Sussex border at Beckley, a character known as Squire Wickham-Martin, one of the last of the family (I believe) who were descended from the Cromwellian General Fairfax. The name 'Squire' was satirical; he was in fact an alcoholic *in extremis*, but in pubs or out, mottled and bottle-nosed as he looked, he retained the somewhat grandiose manner of a Victorian gentleman.

I found him hard-up as usual and anxious to sell some old and valuable books and I bought two car-loads from him including a Speed. I hope I did not take advantage of the old boy. It was a simple equation: he did not want his books and he did want money to pay for his drinks.

Less interesting than such occasional bouts of bookselling were my excursions as a professional lecturer, duly on the directory of these issued by Christina Foyle. It became a nuisance eventually but I did not realize at first how unrewarding it was. I used to lecture with slides which I had made from photos by Douglas Glass about Gypsies or the Circus and nearly always the club or society contracting me was in Northumberlandshire or Dublin or Scotland, somewhere which exhausted my fee to pay the fare. This varied between ten and twenty pounds just as it did for Oscar Wilde seventy years earlier, and although it was an easy job to entertain ladies' luncheon clubs for an hour I would return to London poorer than I set out. Besides, there were mishaps. I more than once forgot which of the two lectures I was due to deliver and brought the slides for the wrong one. On one occasion an old lady sat in the front row and conspicuously snored throughout, because she wanted Gypsies instead of the Circus or vice versa. The best part of it was travelling to unknown and often interesting places, Scarborough, Keswick, Carlisle and Lancashire manufacturing towns. I found a significant fact—that in towns in the South of England it was unsafe to invite questions because someone would begin a long bout of heckling, designed to show that he believed he knew all about the origins of the Romanies or whether Philip Astley really was the father of the English circus, whereas in the North, if people asked a question they really wanted an answer. On the whole lecturing was a waste of time, the audience's and my own, and I could quite believe that it had helped to drive Oscar Wilde to matrimony. The most unpleasant experience I had was finding myself on the same platform with Ruby M. Ayres and Barbara Castle—rather similar in type, I thought. The pleasantest was at Uppingham School.

I do not suppose much of that old type of lecturing persists now, with its dusty parish halls or over the barely cleared table-cloths of a café lunch, in special meeting-places smelling of hastily applied soap to lay the dust, with 'magic lanterns' whose only entertainment was when they 'went wrong', and mayoral introductions—it was, even at that time just after the war, a remnant of Victorian working-class culture or striving upper-class feminism. I imagine it has disappeared, one of the hangers-on, good and bad, which were finally eliminated by television, like the fiction magazines apparently for half-witted semi-illiterates which flourished in scores on railway bookstalls, or like 'musical evenings' at which, incidentally, the untrained performances of amateurs were often better than those of many television artists today.

[3]

Gosh, how I must have worked in those years—though *when* I cannot tell, for I remember chiefly endless amusement. In addition to all the lectures I gave, about fifty, all the broadcasts, more than a score, all the reviews for the *Sketch*, one a fortnight for six years, all the short stories, about eighty, all the articles in newspapers, rather more, all the motoring out of London for literary purposes and all the journeys abroad, I wrote seven novels and five non-fiction books, collected the material for two anthologies and kept up a prodigious correspondence. I do not know how I achieved it, particularly since I was determined to be able to say at the end of my life that I had never published a book, however bad or good it might be considered, which was not the best I was capable of writing at the time. My reputation with my agents was such that when Steinbeck (I think it was) sent in a long commissioned short story to *Lilliput* four and a half thousand words too short so that a story of just that length had to be written before the following week-end, they turned to me and I achieved it with a day to spare, and saw it published in that excellent little magazine, now alas no more.

I felt there was nothing I could not do in the way of writing, speaking or making friends; it was to be three years later that a sudden and savage check came to these, but within yet another year I was away again, adding to my catalogue this series of autobiographical books and four books about wine and three about cookery, plus the novels and non-fiction books I managed, sometimes at the rate of four a year. I am not proud of this overproductivity: I only do not believe that if I had written less I should have written better.

I undertook anything. A department of the Royal Navy concerned with propaganda wanted to make a film about Security and I wrote the script and went down to Portsmouth to see the film. I met the son of Stacey Aumonier, a short-story writer whom I had always admired, and heard that Aumonier's widow, the pianist Gertrude Peppercorn, possessed the outline of a novel which Aumonier had left, and undertook to edit it for publication. I wrote for the *English Novelists Series* a book on Rudyard Kipling. The only line of this which leaves me unashamed was written of *Kim*: 'The reader does not finish this novel, he disembarks from it.' I undertook, and carried out, a pamphlet explaining menu terms for Shell and I completed a History (in forty thousand words) for a firm of timber agents named (if I remember right) Price and Pearce. I made a journey into Wales with a BBC technician to find and do a broadcast about 'true Romanies', who were supposed to follow a clandestine existence in the impenetrable Welsh hills. (We did not find them of course but made do with some *didakai* families on a camping ground.) I was invited to Paris by the Aga Khan who wanted a biography of himself written, particularly by a fellow admirer of the novelist Patrick Hamilton, but found after a number of pleasant talks with the Aga and Begum that he was committed in a contract with American publishers to work with a biographer of their choosing and did not continue with the job. I went down to the hop-gardens of the Weald of Kent to do a broadcast with the pickers for the *Children's Hour* which I enjoyed (nostalgia *and* experience), and completed the libretto of an operatic venture of Maurice Ohana's, the BBC deciding that they thought Maurice's music might be quite good if they could only understand it.

Yet, after all this, with the twelve books I have already mentioned which I wrote during the six years I am recalling, I did not make more than a coal-miner's wage of that time. Before the war from the time I had begun to write, say 1925, to 1940, I did not average three hundred and fifty pounds a year and since that time to the present, say from 1953 to 1973, in which I have written more than forty books, I may have averaged two thousand, including film rights, but this has to be divided because it is the result of the whole working time of Joseph as well as myself. Do you wonder that I make a sound usually described as a hollow laugh when smiling politicians continue to promise year after year to secure for writers a small proportion of the proceeds of books borrowed *free* from lending libraries?

I do not feel self-pity—I am perhaps rather amused in a cynical way when I read in *The Times Literary Supplement* that the number of those who can live entirely by their writings in Great Britain would fit into one not very large room, or that creative writing except for the authors of occasional bestsellers, is rapidly dying out. What else can it do in these days of state-assisted higher education when virtually no one can *choose* writing as a career and expect to make a living from it?

I freely admit that for nearly fifty years I have done what I liked doing best, also that I have kept alive, and enjoyed every moment of it, but I do sometimes wonder what I shall do when I can no longer write several books a year, since it has never been possible to save money and, through a series of mischances, I have almost no National Health pension. I know there are homes for aged printers and pressmen, for I have been asked to subscribe to them. The Arts Council, which has three times turned down my publisher's appeals for me, may help others who have in no way offended its members, who are fortunate enough to have proletarian beginnings, or belong to the PEN or the Authors' Society, or write unreadable books, and I believe there are other public charities. But what, in fact, will I eat, and where may I expect to sleep, when the last Finis is written? Morbid, you say, but you must be prepared to say it a few hundred times to other writers in my approaching situation, even among those not reputed to be prickly. As for the United States of America, I have never written books which Americans view with favour and although no less than fourteen New York publishers have expressed their intention to 'launch' me, they have always given up after one or two books.

But these experiences and apparent misfortunes are in no way rare among writers. Indeed I consider myself lucky to have been able to earn a living for fifty years (with two breaks, one for bookselling and one for six years in the Army) from writing at all. It is surely now for younger writers to mobilize, demonstrate, introduce some violence, do anything that members of other despised trades unsupported by unions have done to secure what I believe is called a fair slice of the cake. But that will never happen so that writers must be reconciled, I suppose, to begging a subsistence from the Welfare State which has held us in contempt.

[4]

Let us return to the more generally interesting aspects of life which showed themselves in those London years. The possession of a car, even of a hundred-pound Opel which had spent the war in an open-ended barn, enabled me to obtain from familiar regions of the Weald of Kent such articles in scarce supply as an over-priced bottle of whisky from a pub, pickled pork from one of the less law-abiding butchers, occasional cartons of cream, and once a quantity of rice. Rice became in fact (what it is for millions of orientals) our vital sustenance, and while Cyril Conolly was obtaining American supplies donated to the needy contributors of *Horizon* I wrote to my agents, who were sometimes my friends, in New York and Buenos Aires. Both Alan Collins and Lawrence Smith sent enough rice for me and Joseph to live on vegetable curry through all the hardest years, and this saved us from experimenting with such emetics as whale-meat and *snoek*. Everyone I knew, including my most improvident Army friends, seemed to have some secret source of supply, the only exceptions, as usual, being the conscientious pensioners and impoverished middle-class ladies who could not afford even to look for relief and sometimes suffered from under-nourishment, while they angrily watched the ludicrous structure of the Festival of Britain using up scarce materials on the South Bank.

Had I been much accustomed, before and during the war, to study with acumen and make predictions with confidence about world happenings, I might have been more disturbed by them now, but I learned long ago not to attempt judgments at the time, for it seemed to me that the slick and knowing gentlemen who predicted exactly what effect events would have were nearly always wrong. I had not a notion about the Chinese Revolution or the Berlin Corridor except that they both seemed to work, or in England about the Squatter Movement, just then at its height, though I vaguely wished it well. I was prescient enough to suspect the African Groundnut Scheme as a big Con, but in my careless mind MacArthur and McCarthy were just a pair of American nuisances.

I could see things closer to home and I have never, before or since, been so angered and shamed by a public event as I was by the judicial murder of the nineteen-year-old Derek Bentley in order to curry favour with the police by that abominable Home Secretary, Sir David Maxwell-Fyfe. I take few public causes to heart but this one has been with me ever since the Speaker refused to allow the matter of Bentley to be debated on the night before his execution, and the last desperate effort of an All-Party deputation of MPs who tried to see Maxwell-Fyfe but failed to move him. Bentley was a Grade IV mental defective and was under arrest at the time that Christopher Craig, his sixteen-year-old companion and leader shot a policeman. I can still see in recollection the pictures of the wretched boy's family on their way to visit him on the eve of his execution.

There have lately been attempts to revive the case by seeking to prove that Craig did not fire the recorded shot, but I do not feel that this was desirable or necessary. Surely it is enough to know that a crazy innocent boy was manœuvred into death for another's crime, and to satisfy what can only be called a thirst for blood.

> Or does the ghost of Bentley bar that way
> Butchered to make a Policeman's Holiday?

I wrote in a long verse satire twenty years later.

As for Maxwell-Fyfe, who not only opposed the abolition of hanging and later introduced the Witch Hunt of homosexuals (both of which ended in legislation to relieve the oppressive measures he supported), my loathing is such that I can feel no sympathy for members of his family still living and do not hesitate to anticipate history by calling him an obscene brute.

Murder cases in those years just after the war seemed to be given more attention than they deserved and even before newsprint control was eased the dailies and Sundays went to town on the case of the psychopathic sex murderer Neville Clevely Heath, and later on his sordid would-be imitator Haigh. Perhaps in the release to the public of such cases after the necessary repressions of war time we felt a sort of relief that murder cases were so comparatively unusual and rare.

[5]

I remember in one of those years the Olympic Games, or a skinflint imitation of them, were held in London. I found my attempts to follow them—never very enthusiastic—faded out altogether as Great Britain won three events against America's thirty-eight. Besides, they were done on the cheap. 'How shall we welcome the foreign teams?' I asked Beverley Nichols.

'Probably by inviting them to a cup of tea with Mrs Braddock,' he suggested. We both remembered better days and would not have minded so much if other countries, belligerent and non-belligerent, were not, as we had observed, enjoying what were called 'good times'.

Not Germany, however, or not just yet. There were shortages greater than our own—a consoling fact to many—and I thought of my German friend of twenty years standing, Ernst Thoma. He had written to me a week or two before the outbreak of war to say that clearly we should not be able to communicate for a time, but that he would get in touch with me when it was all over. He had now done so. He had been wounded on the Russian Front where both his younger brothers had been killed. It was possible, at that time, to pay the travel expenses of Germans invited to English homes and I achieved this with a great deal of form-filling and guarantees.

Ernst arrived and it would have done the heart good of those who held the German *people* responsible for British sufferings in the war to hear what he, on his side, had been through. His mother had died of that old-fashioned incurable malady, a broken heart, after her two younger sons were killed in Russia. She had found the greatest difficulty in forgiving Ernst for surviving them through the lucky chance of having frostbite and wounds together and being sent back to Germany, then under the perpetual tremors of Anglo-American bombing. His wife Clemens had been arrested by the SS and his baby daughter Roswitha had narrowly escaped death from undernourishment. The only tobacco he had smoked for the last two years was from the leaves of *Nicotiana* plants which he had managed to raise in a window-box. He had worked, since his rejection by the army, for sixteen hours every day, and after her release his wife was also conscripted for civilian work. He and his family had, it is true, kept alive somehow, but his envy of what seemed to him England's plenty (in 1948!) was evident. However, he had not broken down, and anyone observing us together, one from each side of the war, would have wondered at our high-spirited enjoyment of London.

Nothing that either of us could say to the other could lessen our mutually ferocious loathing for the man Hitler and for those about him who, according to Ernst, exploited his psychopathic condition. I hoped then, and continue to hope, that mankind will keep a mouthful of spittle for his memory to the end of time.

[6]

My passion for 'keeping in touch' with old friends, by-the-way acquaintances, people with whom I had exchanged conversation on a train, led to some embarrassing and some delightful situations. I told in *The Glittering Pastures* of my first encounter in 1921, that is, at the age of eighteen, with a man over fifty. I had been given two stalls for a musical called *The Great Awakening* and in the bar during one of the intervals I fell into conversation with an urbane and, as it seemed to me, elderly man who was also alone. William Henry Chalmers Roberts was an American who had come to Europe as a War Correspondent in the Balkan War and remaining in London published an English edition of *The World's Work*. He was, in fact, that fabulous being, an *editor*. Grey-haired, clean-shaven, rather bald and dressy he was, I saw at once, entirely at home in the brilliant surroundings which I was so tentatively exploring. With shy courage I asked him if he would see the rest of the show with me, showing him my unused ticket. He was an habitual theatregoer of a kind too rare for the good of the theatre. Living alone in a service flat he would allow himself an evening or two a week free from other engagements, then go to the pit of any theatre where the show was not popular enough for a queue. He liked to go alone; he did not regard the theatre as providing a night out but went as for several decades people went to their local cinema, taking whatever fare was provided. He never booked a seat, and he never, he told me long afterwards, came out before the end. But that night, amused at my invitation, he conceded a point and joined me in the stalls.

When the show was over Chalmers Roberts asked me—casually man to man, as though I was accustomed to such invitations—to come round to his flat for a drink. Ten years before, it seemed, when 'service flats' were rather the thing for bachelors, Ouida heroes, men-about-town, he had taken a long lease on a small one in Jermyn Street, then a smart residential street for just such well-to-do Londoners as he. His sitting-room was decorated—inevitably, I see now—with lacquer and Chinese porcelain and seemed to me splendidly oriental and sophisticated. A whisky-and-soda? Thank you. A cigar? Please. So I sat towards midnight chattering happily, sipping my whisky, feeling, if not perhaps looking, a suave and experienced young man.

What did I do on my return to London a quarter of a century later but find Chalmers Roberts now in his eighties and working in a department of Heinemann's, and ask him to a party? He was, he had once claimed, a first cousin to James

Branch Cabell, which endeared him to me for one of the great enthusiasms of my adolescence had been *Straws and Prayerbooks* and *Beyond Life* and all Cabell's other books. He came and it was with a kind of fascination that I went to dine with him in that same flat in Jermyn Street with the same Chinese porcelain. But he had not aged gracefully (who does beyond eighty?), and was in fact rather a bawdy and undignified old man.

Then, this time from the Argentine past of more than twenty years ago, came 'Bimbo' Beccar Varela, now a very tall very thin and very electric lawyer, as one might have imagined he would be from his aspect as the boy who had edited a paper with me (though I had seen him since then in Buenos Aires in 1936). We had one hurried meeting, scarcely time enough to remember our fortnightly, *La Estrella*, since he had to rush off and dine with one of the frozen meat Vesteys, whose interests he looked after in Argentina. But if there are any readers who have got through *both The Glittering Pastures* and *The Wild Hills* they will know that this was an occasion for me.

Finally there was a meeting with my godmother whom I had not seen for more than a dozen years. It will be hard for any of those born since 1939 to realize what a godmother meant to a child born in a middle-class Edwardian family. The choice was a careful one for the parents, for on it their offspring had to rely for birthday presents and Christmas presents every year, and eventually, if the godparent was all that had been supposed, for a legacy on his or her demise. This led to a good deal of invidiousness in a family like mine in which there were five boys and a girl and the advantages of the various godparents were a matter of boasting and competition.

I had a splendid pair—my godfather being my father's cousin Philip Croft, and the godmother my mother's old friend Bella Whitehead. Magnificent presents used to come from my 'Uncle' Philip, including large toy yacht and a clockwork torpedo boat which actually crossed ponds. Later he gave me— a thrilling present to a boy of sixteen—my freedom to order a fiver's worth of books and I chose The Complete Works of

Francis Thompson in a magnificent buckram binding which I still possess. But I only met him once, a heroic figure in my eyes, because my father had (through his own fault) quarrelled with my great-uncle Septimus Croft, and 'Uncle' Philip died suddenly and young.

Bella Whitehead was a glamorous person when she used to stay with us in my childhood—elegant, sophisticated, charming. Later she read my books and congratulated me on them and while I was in the Army her letters were exhilarating. She lived in what seemed to me a beautiful flat in Hampstead where I was taken as a schoolboy. She and her sister reminded me, I can't say why, of the sisters Schlegel in *Howard's End*, so cultured and up to date she appeared after my dear parents with their philistine 'good taste'.

By the time I visited her after the war she must have been in her late seventies. When I had seen her last she had still moved with grace and spoke musically and without hesitation, but now she had lost her only sister and had left her flat when the bombing started in London and moved to Malvern and it was there I visited her on the occasion of my ridiculous pursuit of Welsh gypsies for a broadcast.

I found her in a Private Hotel. It was a large comfortable well-furnished house with conservatories attached—the very place for a well-to-do septuagenarian spinster who had lived in comfort all her life, but for the Bella Whitehead I remembered, *au fait* with the latest books, knowledgeable about the most publicized musicians, a first-nighter who entertained small discreet conversational parties in her flat, it seemed to me sad, a little stuffy and passé like a once-fashionable parish church. When Bella Whitehead walked slowly into the room, a very aged lady, I realized, perhaps for the first time in my life, that everyone has to become old and die. In people one was constantly with, like one's parents, it is not noticeable. In people who have always seemed old, ever since one met them, like Chalmers Roberts, it makes very little difference. But compared with the Bella Whitehead, whom I had last seen with thick fashionable white hair and smart middle-aged clothes, this frail old lady was a ghost, and she made me realize, as I had never done before, that I too must come to it—though still somewhere in the unseeable future.

In a round thirty years our rôles had been reversed. Now it was I who told her about London doings, reputations and personalities, while she listened to it all with a flush of awakened interest. I think it cheered her to see me and I was glad I went. A year or two later, at a very critical and penurious point in my affairs, she died, and I found she had left me a sum of money. It was the only legacy left specifically to me that I have ever received and as Bella Whitehead had charmed me as a boy, I was brought to a grateful fervour after her death.

[7]

Joseph was entirely at home in London. Up to the time of his arrival, there had been few young Indians and those chiefly university students. The Londoners at that time behaved almost sentimentally with Indians as they did with the Irish, and never, in all his years in England, in spite of later hostility so cleverly depicted by Colin MacInnes, was he ever allowed to feel the faintest touch of embarrassment let alone inimicality. Small wonder that as we have wandered about the world for the last twenty years his dream is always to live in London. He ignores the situation produced by overcrowded immigration, the impossibility of my ever being able to afford to take a flat and live in my own capital city, the occasional manifestations of racialism (a word that scarcely existed then) and says persistently that he would rather live in London than anywhere.

I realized that the poor old London of those days, with half its buildings down and a new breed of criminals in its streets, which to me was a degenerate version of the London I had first known in Edwardian prosperity, was to him and other young immigrants the fabulous London heard of in remote villages of the East or in African forests. He became an Englishman in culture, speech and humour, and better than a European in manners, but he has never outlived the first excitement of the London scene, as many a provincial Englishman has never done. His letters to his home at first were written in the complicated Dravidian script, but he has taught his family to read and write English which has become his language. One of the few (unkind critics may say the *only*) really intelligent, far-seeing and successful things I have done in my life was to invite him to leave his family, his way of life and his background to venture to another continent and adapt himself to it.

Before I close this scandalously miscellaneous and trivial chapter, I want to remember two other small incidents, both in their way typical of those years, though suitably contrasted one with the other. The first was of the world of deserters, bombed-site dwellers, delinquents and—a new word—spivs, the other symbolized that craving for culture, ambition to write, make music or paint which has developed into the pop literature, music and art of today. The first is the story of a burglary, the second of lecturing to a summer course for would-be writers.

The burglary began in one of the pubs in that corner of London I frequented, I cannot remember if it was the Fitzroy, the Wheatsheaf or the Marquis of Granby. I was approached by a young man in the uniform of Polish navy and asked for a drink. He reminded me of those sailors on the Polish ship *Batory* with whom I had played poker while she lay in Glasgow docks. He was an impish young scamp living on his wits, and I knew it perfectly well when I took him back to Doughty Street to hear his story.

It was a picaresque affair as shameless and eventful as the tale of Lazarillo de Tormes and I was vastly entertained by it. It was a few days before Christmas and Micky—Micky Mouse as he appropriately called himself—promised to ring me up during the holiday and give me a second instalment.

I was staying with John Torr* for Christmas and Joseph was also away. When I was phoned in the afternoon it was not by Micky Mouse but by Joseph who had returned to find the flat a shambles. Micky, doubtless homesick for the Christmas spirit, had bluffed the caretaker of the rooms downstairs and persuaded her into handing him over the key. Some clothes and three carefully hoarded bottles of whisky had been stolen with some other odds and ends and two suitcases had been packed ready for removal that night. Micky Mouse had had his fill of cheese.

I had, in a drawer upstairs, a very beautiful French revolver and some ammunition for it confiscated from a Chinese storekeeper in Madagascar and kept deep in a kitbag as I walked through the Customs at Liverpool. It was unusual but handy and such a spectacular weapon that the Rajah of Akalkot† had offered me a thousand rupees for it. I found this had disappeared and decided to dial 999.

The police appeared, of course, the whole incident becoming rather like *Z Cars*, but these were not either the soap opera heroes of television or the amiable if class-conscious bobbies of my boyhood, but a new kind of creature, recruited since the war and accustomed to combat this very outbreak of post-war crime. I had learned to co-operate with the police as part of my Security duties in the Army, but that was in 1940 and 1941, and the whole Force seemed to have changed since the end of the war. I think it is generally recognized that between 1945 and, say, 1960, much of the English police force was at its lowest a blackmailing, thieving, bullying lot of wastrels serving for the sake of the perks and exploiting the reputation for honesty and good nature which their predecessors had guarded ever since the days of the 'peelers'. They belonged to a new type of policeman, drifters out of the Army, NCOs from Detention Barracks, CMP or SIB types or others looking for some alternative to honest work.

Some of those who investigated the crimes of Micky Mouse

*See *The Moon in My Pocket*. †See *The Gorgeous East*.

and who, admittedly, arrested him and his collaborator, beat him up to obtain a statement (as one of them told me), stole in turn the three bottles of whisky which he had stolen from me, and were grossly discourteous and arrogant to everyone connected with the case including the caretaker. When the wretched Micky complained to the Magistrate of his beating up, I remember clearly the scornful tone of the exchange between magistrate and policeman, spoken it seemed as a familiar matter of course.

'Any truth in this, Sergeant?'

'Oh not the slightest, Sir.'

Micky was given six months and recommended for deportation. I was fined a pound for possession of the revolver which I had found under a cushion of the settee.

It was my first but not to be my last encounter with the police during that period of their degradation, and it taught me a great deal. After a succession of prosecutions of individual policemen, investigations by Chief Constables, increases of pay and other measures, things have, I am told, vastly improved. It was not before time.

[8]

The penultimate episode which I feel should be preserved from that period (the last of all is recounted in the final chapter) is lighter-hearted—indeed verges on comedy.

I was invited by an organization existing to hire a huge Derbyshire house which functioned for conventions of every kind, to spend any time I liked there during the ten-day duration of a 'literary course', provided I would give one lecture on the business of writing. The invitation sounded at first so preposterous that I decided to refuse it out of hand, but then I found that L. A. G. Strong, whose work I admired, was to be one of my fellow lecturers and I remembered that I had never seen Derbyshire, and I had not much to do at the time, and the weather was inviting—I accepted.

I found the 'staff room' and was offered, for the only time during my stay, an orange-juice lightly flavoured with gin (a drink which at its best I dislike) and learned about the whole organization. It was run, I was told, on a non-profit basis, the 'lecturers' being offered hospitality but no fee, the 'students' paying a moderate charge for their board and—I feared—the entertainment which I and the others were expected to provide. The staff consisted chiefly of middle-aged ladies of the school matron type, the 'students' when I saw them were not even middle-aged, they were frankly elderly. There must have been over a hundred of them, among them only one young man and a few young girls who had come for the lark; the rest I recognized, like it or not, as my own readers—retired ladies and gentlemen subscribing (in those days) to Boots and other lending libraries.

I gave my lecture, ate in the 'refectory' (ascetically monkish in diet as well as name) and was rather disappointed in L. A. G. Strong whose years as a schoolmaster had left him didactic and dull, not at all as I expected from the author of *Dewer Rides* and *The Brothers*. There were also two writers of books for children, a lady in a peasant shawl and home-made bangles named Alison Uttley, and a businesslike employee of George Newnes and C. Arthur Pearson named Malcolm Savile. But the whole thing was given point and memorability by the presence of one of those professional writers and humorists whom I had so much admired ever since I met Derwent Miall. This was A. A. Thomson who had a considerable reputation as a polished and nutty humorist, a light novelist, a writer for *Punch*, and I believe a cricket commentator.

Luckily I had the Opel with me and it enabled us to ride about the glorious Derbyshire countryside and drink pints in glorious Derbyshire pubs for the rest of our stay. A grand fellow.

CHAPTER TEN

Cinema and Bullring

[1]

IN ALL my life as a writer from the occasion I 'showed up' verses instead of essays at my preparatory school till now, at no time did I become more nearly involved with the stage and cinema than during those years immediately after the war. I was meeting famous actors and actresses at the home of Peter and Molly Daubeny and elsewhere, and became acquainted with those two performers who dominated the quiz games of radio respectively in the 1940s and 1950s, Professor C. E. M. Joad and Gilbert Harding. Joad was a loquacious egotistic man, opinionated away from the microphone as he was in front of it; Harding gave the impression of wandering, though with apparent loud confidence, through a maze in which he had no idea what had happened to him, bemused by success, drink and overwork.

The British films of that time had improved enormously from the upper-middle-class drawing-room dramas or crude melodramas of before the war, and the American musical comedies, *Oklahoma!* and *Annie Get Your Gun* set us all singing or making rude parodies ('The son in the morning and the daughter at night' or 'Doing what comes unnaturally'). There had not been, we agreed, such musicals since Gilbert and Sullivan or the *Geisha*, or the *Belle of New York*, even in the rush of them during and after the *other* war, *Chu Chin Chow*, *No No, Nanette* and the rest. It was a provoking, exciting time for anyone who believed that he could easily turn his hand to a play or a film-script as so many novelists believed. I was not so bemused as that, but I became caught up in several temptations.

I had been fooled by a letter from a literary agent's assistant who told me that a film company in America wanted to base 'a small incident in a film' on a one-act play of mine called *Banquo's Chair*. They offered me about £300 for this seemingly trivial agreement and I accepted while I was still in the Army in India. When I came home I managed to see the film at a small cinema in south-east London. It was a 'second feature' but they had used my entire play almost word for word. What was more, a few years later appeared on television an adaptation of it by Alfred Hitchcock, but it appeared that my contract included television rights and I had no redress. It is long ago and I do not know whose fault it was—that of the agent's assistant or the film-makers, but I do remember my resentment at having been misled and deprived of a reasonable fee for the only film work I had so far sold.

I was not so discouraged by this incident, however, that I could not recognize a chance when I saw it. A man named Hugh Percival, who acted as an assistant or scout for Carol Reed, believed, on the strength of certain novels of mine, that I could write a script for Reed and I went to his house, then in Chelsea, to discuss it. It happened that on the same day there had arrived from Austria the old man and his grand-daughter or grand-niece, whom Carol had heard playing in a café the 'Harry Lime' tune at the time he was making *The Third Man*. They were practising in a studio and I thus heard that mysteriously maddening piece of music which was to drill the ear-drums of the whole world with its unforgettable theme, and became far better known and enduring than Graham Greene's story, Reed's direction, Orson Welles' acting, or any part of that sensational film.

Percival had not only picked me but selected a story for me to script, a rather flat minor novel of Maurice Hewlett (1861–1923) called *The Spanish Jade*. I worked on this for a month, having frequent conferences with Carol Reed in Doughty Street and elsewhere but the novel, or my lack of confidence in it, beat me and I knew that what I had done was not good enough. Beyond a meeting with Alexander Korda, and many pleasant discussions with Carol, and a fee for my wasted time, I got nothing from the experience and resolved that I would never try to write a script of my own books, even if one of them was to be filmed. I kept that promise so that when a few years later, after I had moved to Tangier, I sold the film rights of *Seven Thunders* I did not even come to England while the film was being made with Stephen Boyd, Kathleen Harrison, Anna Gaylor, Tony Wright, James Robertson Justice and all. I have never seen the film in English and have kept away from the filming of several of my books since then.

But now there was a special reason for trying to do something with a play. I met again after some twelve years, the film star Douglass Montgomery, not to be confused with any other Montgomery. (This was *Douglass*, once known as Kent Douglas.) I stress the film star bit because that is what he had been—one of those Hollywood Olympians who in earlier days did bestride the narrow world like a Colossus. He had been an actor on the New York stage at sixteen and reached the height of his success when he starred with Margaret Sullavan in *Little Man What Now?* and in a film version of the life of Stephen Collins Foster, the creator of half the 'folk' music of America.

In the days when I first met him, 1936 or so, I was young enough to feel some of that kind of hero-worship which half the population gave to film stars, something entirely different from the critical grudging admiration which television actors earn for themselves today by a fine performance. Douglass believed I could write a play for him then. I still have the 300-word telegram suggesting revisions which he sent to me in mid-Atlantic when I left for Buenos Aires for the second time. The strange thing was that now, ten years later when I met him, he still believed I could do so, and I was still so overcome by his magnetism that I agreed to work on an idea which he liked. So much did he seem to be the most brilliant and attractive of all young actors—he was still around thirty—that I did not dream of insisting on a contract but in a series of summer afternoons worked after lunch with Douglass in his suite in the Dorchester until I had produced a play which pleased him, a modern version of the Tichbourne Scandal, with Douglass as an American sailor unwillingly claiming his right to an English manor.

But Douglass in spite of his notable good looks and natural talent was a tragic figure who could never recapture his first success and suffered ghastly psychoses and neuroticisms on account of it. Just at that time he was offered and accepted the London lead in *Detective*, a play which he made a huge success in New York, but a few days before the first night he developed a nervous form of laryngitis and failed to make a success of what should have been a part full of shouting and bullying, and an opportunity for him to return to full stardom. He believed in the play I had written for, and partly with him, but no one had the faith in him that was needed to put on a play for Douglass Montgomery by an unknown play-wright. (Besides, it may have been lousy; I can't remember now.)

Douglass, so far as I know, never achieved the dramatic glories of his youth in a play or a film, though I believe that after I left England in 1954 he returned to America where he had some success on television. I know only hearsay details of how he died in the 1960s—he was afflicted by some rare form of endermic cancer and I cannot help wondering whether this too was the result of a psychosis. I loved and admired him for thirty-five years and the death of his art, and his own early death, still seem to me a very real tragedy.

[2]

The invitation to work on a film when it came was not meant for a writer at all. My agents had heard that a multi-national film company with multi-national stars intended to make a film from a short story of Stendhal's (was it *Le Coffre et le Revenant*?) which was to go forth as *The Tyrant of Toledo*. They had engaged Henri Decoin, a very experienced and resourceful director, and as stars Pedro Armendariz, a Mexican Indian by origin who was then very popular, and Alida Valli, fresh from her triumph in *The Third Man*. The film was to be made in four languages at the same time, or in successive takes according to the nationality of the actors, English (Armendariz spoke as an American), French (the young leading man whose name I forget was French), Italian (Alida Valli was to use both her own language and English) and Spanish (most of the minor actors were Spanish). The film was to be made in Toledo, then in the Madrid studios of Chamartin, and finally in Paris.

This unusual venture was to go into production almost immediately and as Alida Valli insisted that someone should check her English pronunciation, the tall young Russian Jew who was making the film had sent urgently to London to find someone to do this.

'If you consider it,' said a woman at my agents, 'all I can promise you is a good holiday. There won't be much work and all the company offers is a tenner a week and your hotel bill. But it's the sort of thing you might enjoy.'

I agreed and having at last sold the Opel and bought a large four-year-old Renault I set off to drive down to Spain by a route which (although I did not know it) I was to cover many times in the years following.

It was early summer and France seemed very young and alive and refreshing as I ran through the countryside which still seemed unchanged since before the war. I reached Roquefort and stayed a night with Robert and his family, then through Biarritz to climb the rainy hills to San Sebastian. I stopped a night at Burgos, delighting as usual in the Spanish scene and people. My recent visits seemed to have been dog-on-a-lead affairs of one day ashore with the inevitable anticlimax of a return to the ship, but now I was care-free among the people I loved. I remember going into a *peluqueria* (that handsome and historical word for a hairdresser's) and finding that the barber, like so many Spaniards, wanted to talk about bull-fighting and was delighted to find an Englishman in his chair whose conversation could range from the fabulous Joselito to young Litri, even though I knew nothing about Manolete whose bright star had risen and set during the Second World War.

In Madrid I had calls to make. Richard Blake Brown's young nephew Richard was taking a course in hotel-keeping which had brought him to the Palace Hotel in Madrid, then the most noisily acclaimed hotel, and I found him there, dressed in the black jacket and striped trousers of his profession to be. I had also brought with me a grubby piece of paper on which was written in unformed handwriting the address of Pepe the onetime stowaway. I traced him to a suburb called Carabanchel and arranged to meet him a few days later.

I found the film company in the Hotel Carlos Quinto at Toledo, the best hotel then—and I daresay still today—in that most exciting city. The Carlos Quinto was no vast luxury hotel but it had a fine lounge and dining-room over it, decorated with some imagination, and a score or two of comfortable bedrooms. With French devotion to the importance of status and precedence, it had been arranged that the director, stars and a group of Spaniards who had money in the project, were accommodated here while the rest of the company, cameramen, technicians, and character actors were at another hotel. I never quite knew what all the Spaniards were doing on the set or why some of them turned up on every occasion. Among them was a middle-aged poet of some reputation—though I did not understand why until one day, he addressed the smoked ham, the *jamon serrano*, traditionally one of the most popular and perfect delicacies in Spain, with *unas disquisiciónes*, a quite spontaneous tribute to the slices on his plate which introduced a great deal of Spanish history and literature, and lasted for almost ten delightful minutes of sheer rhetoric. There was also a middle-aged lady intellectual who like the poet seemed to have no connection with the film.

Henri Decoin was in charge and left no doubt of it in anyone's mind. He was a grand old fellow who at sixty-eight used to walk round the studio floor on his hands and had been married to Daniele Darrieux. He spoke no Spanish; indeed one of the peculiarities of that international collection was that none of them spoke more than two languages and most of them only one. The French spoke no Spanish the Spanish no French. Alida Valli spoke good English and my intended function was totally unnecessary but she spoke no Spanish and none of the rest of them spoke Italian. I was the only person on the set—but *was* I on the set?—who could speak Spanish, French and English and found myself in danger of being co-opted as an interpreter.

Fortunately I was saved from that and everything else unpleasant when I saw the English script. Who had translated it from what language? Whoever it was had been an illiterate or as the Spanish say more descriptively, an *analfabeto*. I told the Russian producer that I proposed to do it completely afresh. Henri Decoin said it was a good idea but doubted whether I should get paid for my work. The Spaniards took no part in the discussion—they were not interested in the English version. I thought the whole thing was amusing. It would mean very little work (as I measured work) and I was being agreeably entertained and I had not been paid with living expenses since I had come out of the Army. I saw that I was going to enjoy myself and I certainly did. It was almost as amusing as travelling with Rosaire's Circus before the war.

So this, I thought, kept awake by the church-bells on my first night in Toledo, was a film unit. It could not, of course, be anything like an ordinary film unit but then I realized that there is no such thing and every production has its own form of eccentricity. The actors here might be of several nationalities but they had been collected from four countries to make what they could of a somewhat over-eventful costume drama. Or rather what Henri Decoin intended that they should make. He was the only one of us to have the least idea of what it was all about.

CINEMA AND BULLRING

The story illustrated an incident during the Napoleonic wars in Spain. It had everything in it—a congregation of villagers for a marriage ceremony for which a disused church had been rented and a local crowd had been conscripted at a few pesetas a day, scenes in old castles, an implied rape of Alida Valli by Pedro Armendariz, a hangman and a fully displayed hanging, a lover imported into Alida Valli's apartment in a chest—the idea from which this macabre miscellany had started—duels, hold-ups, highwaymen, soldiers in contemporary uniforms, inns with comic fat innkeepers, a murder, and an old coach driven at dusk across the hills round Toledo.

The lack of a common language between director and cast led to some embarrassing incidents. The Spaniards who supplied the larger part of the cast numerically speaking, had engaged a well-known local character-actor, considered a star in Spain, as an innkeeper who had to speak two words, '*Si señor!*' while he drew a jug of wine for the young lover meeting Alida Valli in his inn. The actor was determined to make the most of it and all of us who had seen so much incident, character and dialogue to so little purpose were alarmed to find the actor, a large fat man, suddenly turning his words and actions into a *part*. '*Si señor!*' he began, rising to his feet and starting to waddle across the floor, '*Si señor!*' he said a dozen times before the young lover got his wine, repeating the words with every possible change of emphasis, breathlessness, servility, comedy and good-humour, because they were the only words allotted to him. He was a famous clowning comedian and everyone on the set began to laugh.

Except Henri Decoin, who was trying to make a coherent film.

'Tell him,' he said with a spine-chilling brevity, 'just to bring the wine.'

As a snub it was monumental, and I suffered in sympathy with the old Spanish star.

[3]

The Toledo scenes were all shot in old mansions in the town, several of which had been hired from the State. Toledo was full of them and although tourists and sight-seers, chiefly American at that time, came in fair numbers to Toledo they stayed only a few hours to see the El Greco paintings and cathedral or buy a few pieces of metal, modern souvenirs supposed to inherit some of the art of the ancient sword-makers. The atmosphere of history was so heavy about one that the six weeks I spent there were not sufficient to gain more than a breath of Toledo's past. It is of 'immemorial antiquity', a stronghold of the Carpentari, a Phoenician trading centre, later occupied (in 193 BC) by the Romans. It became an important centre of Christianity till Musa conquered it in 712 and under the Moors it became a city of art and commerce in which members of the Jewish colony were protected, among them Rabbi ben Ezra. Recaptured in 1085 by Alfonso de Leon y Castilla, it was the chief city of Christian Spain until Felipe II moved the capital to Madrid in 1560. The past is so insistently about one, in the Plaza Zocodover, in the narrow streets, in the unspoiled façades of mediaeval houses, in works of art, that it becomes oppressive, and one is prone to an almost hysterical excitation if one is shown yet another El Greco or one of Toledo's masterpieces by Goya, Titian and Rubens.

But I was supposed to be concerned with the making of a historical film and was perhaps more moved by the modern story of the heroic Nationalist resistance in the Alcazar which lasted for seventy days of stringent siege. The part-ruined building was only a few score yards above our hotel. The famous story of Colonel Moscardo is vouched for by Hugh Thomas, but is worth recalling yet again after more than thirty years.* Heroic gestures of this kind might have been

*Hugh Thomas, *The Spanish Civil War*, p. 203. "The most celebrated incident of this period in the Spanish War occurred, however, at

CINEMA AND BULLRING

expected of the Civil War in Spain and there were plenty on both sides, but this has a *caballerosidad* of its own which belongs not to Don Quixote himself but rather to those books of chivalry which he studied.

Quite apart from the antiquity of its buildings, Toledo as a city had a certain individual charm and I fear to return there now, more than twenty years later, to find perhaps that the Carlos Quinto Hotel is a draw-up for coaches—I prefer the word char-à-bancs, for that is what they are—that the Plaza Zocodover may have lost its shady arcades and that narrow streets have been widened for the convenience of the almighty motor-vehicle. I am sure I should not find that milk-stall in the plaza where I used to go with Pedro Armendariz to consume a curious drink of iced milk and coconut which he had discovered and professed to enjoy and I might even find the old Moorish bridge over the Tagus enlarged for traffic. Nor, today, would I persuade a tile-maker, the father of a young plaza acquaintance, to undertake to make a name plate for the house which I had just bought—with a mortgage—on the Kent and Sussex border, and in the brilliant blue which has been used for decoration in Spain since the Moorish conquest, produce an oblong

---

Toledo. From Madrid the Minister of Education, the Minister of War, and General Riquelme had been furiously telephoning Colonel Moscardo, commander of the Nationalist garrison still holding out in the Alcazar, in an attempt to persuade him to surrender. Finally, on July 23, Candido Cabello, a leader of the militia in Toledo, telephoned Colonel Moscardo to say that if Moscardo did not surrender the Alcazar within ten minutes he would shoot Luis Moscardo, the Colonel's son, whom he had captured that morning. 'So that you can see that's true, he will speak to you,' added Candido Cabello. Luis Moscardo then uttered the single word 'Papa' over the line. 'What is happening, my boy?' asked the Colonel. 'Nothing,' answered the son, 'they say they will shoot me if the Alcazar does not surrender.' 'If it be true,' replied Colonel Moscardo, 'commend your soul to God, shout *Viva España* and die like a hero. Goodbye my son, a last kiss.' 'Goodbye father,' answered Luis, 'a very big kiss.' Candido Cabello came back on the telephone, and Colonel Moscardo announced that the period of grace was unnecessary. 'The Alcazar will never surrender,' he remarked before replacing the receiver. Luis Moscardo was in fact killed on August 23. The Alcazar remained besieged."

of tiles naming *The Long House* which remains beside the front entrance to that lost home of mine to this day.

Just as I began to feel like an old inhabitant of Toledo, the Unit moved to Madrid where we should work in the Chamartin studios.

[4]

Meanwhile during a visit to Madrid I had seen Pepe the stowaway. He was working with a group of youths, popularly called *The Bicycle Thieves* from the Italian film, who were employed to deliver messages by bicycle all over Madrid, there being no Special Messenger service attached to the Post Office. Almost unknown to the public it was a hopeless proposition and I was not surprised when the organizer of it soon after absconded, leaving Pepe and the rest without their last week's money and without a job.

But his office was in a seven-floor building in the Gran Via and the three upper floors of this were occupied by a hotel named the San Francisco. It was at that time a rather elegant little hotel with only a bar and an office in the entrance hall and some twenty or thirty newly furnished and upholstered bedrooms, each with a bath and endless hot water. Just the place for me, away from the rest of the Unit, whose members had ceased to be the interesting oddities they had seemed at first and were occupied in obscure bickerings. The French, though remaining courteous, regarded the Spaniards as amateurs; the Spaniards had begun to resent the French, and both would certainly have resented the English if there had been any in the cast. When Decoin wanted a considerable change of dialogue he asked the Spaniards to suggest its wording and also asked the French who were mostly cameramen and mechanicians, and me.

'What a language English is for films,' he said as he looked over the five pages of dialogue the Spanish had submitted, full of flowery phrases and verbose romanticism. 'It can all be said in six words.' Which is more or less what I devoted to it, while the French version had that peculiar sound of tearfulness which one finds in so much French film dialogue. The fact that Henri Decoin dismissed these only added to, and brought me into, the growing strain in the unit, not an uncommon phenomenon, I am told, half way through a film.

But the San Francisco Hotel suited me well and Pepe came up in the lift at all times of the day to see if there was 'anything he could do for me', remembering still, from that initial incident and to this day, my casual intervention when he was a stowaway.

Madrid was then a delightful city. You could motor about it and leave your car almost anywhere without trouble or sit on the uncrowded terraces of the cafés in the Gran Via and be drawn into conversations that lasted through the warm night. My Renault was a model made for England with the steering wheel on the right, which brought me cheek by jowl with the drivers of cars beside me and more than once I enjoyed slanging matches with offending taxi-drivers, abuse being a form of Spanish in which I was skilled. Spanish brandy, not nearly so bad as its later reputation, cost then about five shillings a bottle, and a large measure in a café (with soda if you drank it so) less than a shilling. There were comparatively few foreigners of any kind about the streets, certainly less than in any other West European capital, and I wondered later, from the city of recent years, so much less Spanish, so teeming with tourists and so blocked with motor traffic, if I or my English friends fully appreciated it then. *Après nous le deluge* we ought to have said every minute of every day in that enchanting summer.

Rumour that I had found myself a good hotel spread in the Unit and before long Pedro Armendariz moved there. His arrogance and pugnacity had caused him to be arrested for a night and a desperate crew had to bail him out in time for the next day's filming. He was quiet enough at the San Francisco.

I learned more about Spain and the Spanish from this visit

than from any previous one. A small national lunacy I discovered was that when any marriage was in prospect, the first article that had to be provided for the future home was one of those usually hideous glass ceiling lights, with brass bands and crystal pendants made of cheap glass, in those days considered an essential for marital happiness. I passed a shop of these stalactites and discovered that among the least popular models could be found one or two of such simplicity, such popularly unacceptable austerity, that they began to resemble the English chandeliers of a century of two ago. They were cheap by any standard and I succeeded in selecting one without any brass or coloured glass or elaborate design and paid £3 for it. It is amusing to remember that when my furniture was sold a few years later it appeared in the catalogue as 'antique cut-glass chandelier', and fetched £34.

As a good conventional Hispanophil (or is there a contradiction in those terms?), I wanted to see the Escorial. Later I completed the trio of Spain's wonders with the Alhambra and Montserrat and I am not among those foolishly pretentious people who voice esoteric detraction of the great creations of mankind merely because they are commonly admired. I find the Taj Mahal swimmingly beautiful in spite of the embroidered cushion covers and alabaster models of it in the tourist shops of Bombay, and the Parthenon, the Colosseum, Versailles and the rest make me choke back tears by their separate splendours. So the Escorial had not a shade of disappointment for me. In two qualities, its grandeur and its beauty, it seemed all-surpassing as I spent a whole summer day under its shady arches and faraway roofs. It seemed to have all the magnificence of the greatest days of Spain for they started to build it when Cervantes was a boy and the last stone of the Cathedral was laid before he died.

[5]

Pepe came with me everywhere and showed me aspects of Madrid which I should never have seen without him, as a young Cockney might have revealed London to an inquisitive foreign writer. How would I have discovered the supremely good shellfish restaurant of O. Pote, hidden as it is behind a noisy bar littered with fish-heads, and dense with tobacco smoke? How could I have found the eating houses of the University students, rackety with seditious talk, or the quiet streets in which particular trades and handicrafts traditionally flourished? How would I have seen one of Madrid's queer bars, where the *maricónes* were of such effeminacy that they outraged even American drag queens—or one of the bars near the Puerto del Sol which was used exclusively (or very nearly so) by bullfighters so that one might meet them past present and to come?

But that brings me to bullfighting, and I shall talk about it without wasting time on much argument. I have long learned that English people who read in the potted paragraphs of their newspapers of the massed and motorized murder of thousands of their fellow human beings, who accept the abominable cruelties of intensive cattle and bird breeding in which creatures born to freedom and sunlight are kept in darkened cells for the whole of their life, who approve of men tearing away the gills of fish by what is called the contemplative pastime of angling, who, finally, pay to watch two men trying to kill one another in the boxing ring or pretending to do so by wrestling, yet who regard as a personal affront the traditional *fiesta brava* of their neighbours. Few Englishmen or Americans who spend a holiday in Spain fail to see a bullfight 'just out of curiosity', because 'one should see it at least once', because their neighbours at home saw one last year or because, as animal-lovers, they feel they should witness the terrible thing for themselves. (There are none more ferocious than animal lovers.) Without any of these forms of hypocrisy let me declare that I have been an *aficionado* since adolescence and continue as such today.

But in that year a new element came into my *afición*, since I became more or less closely acquainted with several bullfighters. While the film unit was at Toledo *El Litri*, as Miguel Baez was called, that most heroic of the *novilleros* of that year, gave one of those superb performances by which he broke Belmonte's 1919 record, taking part in 114 *novilladas* in one year. On the Sunday morning before the fight he came into the bar of the Carlos Quinto with a number of his followers and for some reason chose to come up and speak to me. Whether it was the English accent with which I spoke Spanish or whether he was bored by the members of his *cuadrilla* I cannot tell, but on my side I make no excuse for being delighted by this. As John Marks wrote—'For sheer intoxication the bullfighter's glory eclipses that of the champion athlete or the film-star and is comparable only to the triumphs of the greatest national heroes. He is a boy of humble origin, transplanted in adolescence by his own tenacious endeavours, at physical risk to himself, from poverty—most often abject poverty—into a fabulous paradise of wealth, women, praise, and power. At sixteen or twenty he is a conquering caliph, with the world at his feet. And yet, by some strange effect of his vocation and breeding, almost invariably this dignified Spanish urchin will remain unspoilt. Sometimes such a superman succumbs to the vices of vanity and envy, but he will be the exception among his colleagues, who normally betray no trace of arrogance, vulgarity, or affectation in private life, however flamboyant their behaviour in the ring may be.'

Litri certainly remained unspoilt. He might have been a young shop assistant or employee for all the vanity or self-importance he showed. We talked for half an hour, during which time none of his followers, or indeed anyone else, presumed to approach him. Then he had to leave to prepare for the ring and we arranged to meet again. I assured myself that *but for his fame* and the spectacular means by which he had

CINEMA AND BULLRING

gained it, he might have been any warm and well-mannered young Spaniard, but this was not quite true. I could not disassociate him from his public glory and felt as pleased with myself as any social climber at being singled out for his acquaintanceship. Naif, perhaps, but understandable. If, as John Marks also said, *Litri's* 'grave fantastic magnetism provoked the frenzy of the mob' how was I, an *aficionado* in my forties, to escape it?

From that I went on to meet another young *novillero* in Madrid. The home of my one-time stowaway, a tiny but hospitable cottage in a row of such, was in the suburb of Carabanchel, famous for its prison. The cottage consisted of a single floor of three rooms with a vine-covered *patio* behind it. (The vine spread to benefit the neighbours in three such houses.) Pepe's father was lame, an accident at work long ago had brought him a post as a woodwork instructor in a school. Pepe's mother was a typical Madrileña, shrill, witty, sometimes abusive and always hospitable.

A few yards away from this little house, to which I went to drink coffee on Sunday afternoons, was a bullring, the lesser one of the two in Madrid, named—I think—Vista Allegre. It was less crowded and far less expensive than the great bullring of the capital and *novilladas* were held there rather than *corridas* of fully-fledged bullfighters. There I was able to take ring-side seats in the shade, a luxury nowadays so highly priced that few can afford it, though somehow they are always full.

It is the habit, after the initial parade led by the *aguaciles* for which the *matadores* wear all their brilliant garments *de luces* which may cost two or three hundred pounds, to disperse behind the barrier and sling their gala capes to friends in the front row for safe-keeping. The friend accepts the charge knowing that it may represent a large part of the *novillero's* worldly goods, and spreads it over the ledge in front of him.

On a Sunday afternoon during my first weeks in Madrid the Vista Allegre was sparsely occupied for a *novillada* of three unknown young aspirants. One of them, a blond boy who had only recently come to Madrid and had no friends, handed his cape to me. We exchanged smiles, I said *'Con suerte, amigo!'* and an indifferent *corrida* began. The young *matador* managed his first bull pretty well and was applauded, but his second bull was an ugly brute who tossed him over his shoulder, so that he had to be carried down to the dressing station. One of his *cuadrilla* collected his cape.

A talkative man who came from the bullfighter's native town of Huelva went to enquire about him and returned to tell me that he was not badly damaged, and that if I liked he would take me to see him. A cloak *de luces* being bond enough I went, and thereafter met young Miguel on various occasions. I found, as I had rather expected, that he and I and most members of his community had only one subject of conversation, *los toros*. Admittedly this was a topic of wide range, the history, the personalities, the events, the heroes, the breeders and the rivalries of the ring but never its hazards, which simply were not mentioned. With Miguel and through him I met a number of young enthusiasts of bullfighting and from their talk I made and published two short stories, though never a novel on the subject, which I felt would demand more of my lifetime than I was prepared to give.

[6]

Most memorable of all the *corridas* I have ever attended was one which came like a miracle to Segovia, to which I had gone partly to see its buildings and its remarkable Roman aqueduct (the bridge portion of which, crossing the valley into the city, is $8\frac{1}{2}$ hundred yards long and is in working order to this day), and partly to see a *novillada* promised for that day. But all aqueducts are very much alike and as I looked at it I was thinking of the bullfight in which a certain Jumillano was to perform for the last season as a *novillero*, since next year he would become a *matador de toros*.

We were three, Richard Brown, Pepe the stowaway and I, and we drove in a north-easterly direction from Madrid over the *sierras* on whose slopes were the cool summer residences of rich Madrileños, to Segovia. We lunched outside a restaurant from which we could look up to the towering aqueduct, then moved through gathering and excited crowds to our places in the *sombra*. Jumillano, a tall dark young man, was the third and the sixth to fight and I forget who were his confrères. Some interest was attracted by Franco's daughter who occupied a box, and the air of expectation before the *paseo* mounted almost to breaking-point.

At first the *novillada* seemed almost commonplace. The first three bulls were dispatched without any special finesse or exhibition, one of the bullfighters earning an ear for a smooth and unhesitating kill, but nothing to rouse any violent enthusiasm. The second three, including the sixth killed by Jumillano, were rather better but still not ecstatically good and we and everyone else in the ring felt a shade disappointed.

Then happened a thing most wonderful to me who knew no precedent and had never seen such an event in a bullring before. Jumillano went out and saluted before the President's box.

'He's asking for a seventh bull!' people were saying all around us. He was. That very rare privilege which may be accorded to a bullfighter if he has not been given a chance to excel by the two bulls allotted to him was being demanded. He would fight the seventh bull without monetary award, but when this happens it is usually a splendid event.

In this case it was all that any man could ask. From the first *veronica* one knew that Jumillano was to dominate his animal, a *toro bravo* exactly suited to his exalted purpose. He played it almost disdainfully for a few moments and when the *picadores* prepared to come out on their wretched horses he waved them back. No one was going to touch this bull but himself and he would not have it weakened for the final encounter. He placed all three pairs of *banderillas* himself, again refusing that the *banderilleros* of his own *cuadrilla* should interfere. He then commenced a *faena* of such incredible skill and courage that the whole crowd became hoarse with cheering and shouting 'Olé!' and a man near to us had tears running down his cheeks. By this time I knew that I was witnessing one of those moments of perfection, those supreme triumphs which I might never have the good fortune to see again.

When Jumillano came to kill it was with brevity and sureness, a clean pass running in deep between the shoulders which tumbled the bull over instantly without fuss or stumbling. This was it, this was classic and flawless perfection, this is what we all waited and longed for in endless *corridas* and might see perhaps only once or twice in a lifetime. The crowd yelled deafeningly and long, the President ordered both ears, the tail and all four hooves to be given to Jumillano and the din grew as he commenced his triumphal circling of the arena.

We made our way silently to our car and I for one was repressing tears. None of us spoke till we had travelled ten miles, and then it was of other matters since what we were feeling inside us was inexpressible.

L'Envoi

I REGRETFULLY went back to Paris and selected one among a number of young men who wanted to dub the part of the French lover in the film. This was rather harrowing; I would never have guessed there were so many Americans in Paris who were anxious to work for so little. I learned that the nearly illiterate version of the film, which I had discarded, had been made by two of them and I was not surprised when these two thought that a candidate who spoke with a most hideous enunciation was right for dubbing the part. They grew hostile when I insisted on a quiet New Englander, who did the job most successfully. I found the whole business of dubbing into English strange and interesting and took pleasure in selecting words with the right labials and dentals to match those used in French or Spanish. It meant a couple of weeks' work in the studios opposite the Renault island in the Seine, and the producer had grown so appreciative by this time that he hired a car for me to go to and fro from my hotel.

This hotel had been found for me by Maurice Ohana, who lived not far away in the Rue de Rennes. It was called the Bellechasse and I bless its memory since it had all the essentials —it was clean and cheap, with plenty of hot water and it had freedom of entry alone or accompanied at all times of night. Also it was near St Germain des Prés, which was not then such a coach station for tourists as it is today, and there were excellent little *bistros* within reach of it.

This film period followed me. I was scarcely home when I received another invitation from a department of the great firm of Pathé to script an English version of an Indian film. It appeared that the Hindu husband of a famous Indian girl star thought it would please her to work in a European setting and I crossed, this time with Joseph, to write the story. As anyone knows who saw Indian films of that time (not so common today), they had to be a mixture of Rolls-Royce cars, palaces full of lovely dancers, an element of the supernatural such as a wizard in a cave who turned people into animals, handsome young men who wore beautiful clothes and at the drop of a hat would break into an interminable song or agile display of dancing, and a touch of Hindu mythology. I could manage the Rolls-Royce and the lovely dancers in action, but broke down over the wizardry and early deism which followed them and *could* not find a way of bringing in a nuclear submarine on which the star's husband was particularly keen. So having received a fair portion of my promised fee and left it in a strong-box in a Paris bank (one *never knew* at that time), I returned to England. Paris had never been more exciting or full of temptations and I regretted leaving it.

Perhaps if I had known all that lay ahead for me I might never have done so.